Healing with Flower and Gemstone Essences

by
Diane Stein

THE CROSSING PRESS
FREEDOM, CALIFORNIA

For Sue

For information on bulk purchases or group discounts for this and other Crossing Press titles, please contact our Special Sales Manager at 800-777-1048.

Healing and medicine are two very different disciplines, and the law requires the following disclaimer. The information in this book is not medicine but healing, and it does not constitute medical advice. In case of serious illness consult the practitioner of your choice.

ISBN 0-89594-856-7

Contents

DIAGRAMS

Acknowledgments

I would like to offer special thanks to several women. Carolyn Taylor has tested my flower essences and used them from the beginning. Karen Silverman and Corinne Nichols have encouraged both my essence making and flower gardening, and also tested many of the results. The input and validation of these women has been highly important to my continuing the work.

Robyn Zimmerman has added many new meanings and uses to my flower essence combinations, including an extensive list of physical body indications for the essences I've made. Robyn and Bob Zimmerman have also started the *Essential Reiki Journal* and are now using it to make my flower and gemstone essences available for sale.

Thanks also to Cyndi Barnes of The Crossing Press for helping with the Latin plant names and for total book production. Elaine Gill has tested and encouraged my essence making, besides making my books possible. Thanks too, to Jane Lazear, Karen Narita, and the rest of the folks at The Crossing Press.

Flowers unfold slowly and gently, bit by bit in the sunshine, and a soul, too, must never be pushed or driven but unfolds in its own perfect timing to reveal its true wonder and beauty.

Eileen Caddy,
The Findhorn Garden

Take time to study flowers. Feast your senses and your soul on their colors, textures, fragrances and gestures. Attune yourself to their delicate energy. Every flower is a doorway into another realm, leading to inspiration, wisdom, healing and joy. Enter in!

Debra Eisenmann and
Heidi Eisenmann-Jones,
Ozark Flower Essences

Why Flowers?

Our Goddess Earth is stocked with every type of green life imaginable. Plants provide food for people and animals, shelter and building materials, and medicines to heal wounds and dis-eases. Plants create the oxygen that supports life on Earth, and they breathe the carbon dioxide we exhale as waste. They are primary creators of the ecology and beauty of the planet. Without green life there would be no human or animal life, no insects, birds, or other living things. The Earth would rapidly become uninhabitable. Yet, most people today are aware only of the few varieties of plants that provide food and the few varieties of the trees and flowers that provide beauty around their homes. People today no longer pay attention to the land and the plants that support our lives.

Primarily because of this shift of attention, the Earth and the people and animals who live here are in dire need of healing. By cutting down the rain forests and turning what bit of wilderness that still remains into cities and shopping malls, dozens of plant species are lost permanently. Also lost are habitats for wildlife, birds, and insects, the cures for dread dis-eases, and the stability of the planet's climate and atmosphere.

Stripping the Earth of plant life strips our own means of survival, and the extinction of flower species reduces the joy and beauty of the Earth.

Today's plants are bred for commercial convenience, rather than nutrition, beauty, or variety. They are genetically engineered so that they need chemical fertilizers and pesticides. Fruits and vegetables are picked before they are ripe, so that they will withstand handling and travel without bruising or deterioration. They also may be subject to long storage and chemical treatment before they appear on the table. Commercial food and garden plants are bred for standardized color, size, and growth patterns, with no deviation tolerated. Of the thousands of varieties that may exist, say, of corn or string beans, only a few are still cultivated as food; the rest will eventually become extinct. The tragic Irish potato famine occurred because only one variety of potato was being planted, one susceptible to the blight. Only eight potato varieties are commonly grown in the United States today. Also, the roses and sweet peas that grew in our grandmothers' gardens may no longer be available to us.

However, you can still buy or get old-time plants if you look for them. Wildflowers still grow on open land and will creep into cultivated lawns, and people still share cuttings and seeds from their gardens. The work of organizations like Seeds of Change (POB 15700, Santa Fe, NM 87506-5700), Heirloom Seeds (POB 245, W. Elizabeth, PA 15088-0245), and Shepherd's Garden Seeds (30 Irene St, Torrington, CT 06790-6658) help to preserve older varieties of flowers, herbs, and vegetables. These are called heritage or heirloom plants. Organic gardening with these stronger, time-tested varieties is gaining popularity and is another method of healing the Earth.

People who have begun to pay attention to the land, to heal Goddess Earth by protecting her plants, are reclaiming lost knowledge and old ways. Over the last thirty years, beginning with the Back-to-the-Earth movement of the 1960s, several important groups have brought planetary awareness to the forefront. These groups include the Earth-First! ecology movement, organic farming, and Wiccan, New Age, and Women's Spirituality movements. Here are some of the major findings of these movements:

1) Organically grown foods from natural plant varieties are healthier to eat and more vigorous than commercially farmed foods. They also nurture the planet.

2) Herbs are as effective or more effective in healing disease than prescription drugs. They do no have the chemicals' side effects and subsequent damage.

3) Flowers provide healing as do food plants and herbs.

4) Healing the planet heals all who live on it.

Healing with flowers, particularly through the vibrational method of flower essences, is the subject of this book. I hope to return flower essences to daily use as healing tools and promoters of well-being. The countless varieties of flowers, especially in a homegrown garden or in the wild, provide an avenue (similar to the growing of herbs) for human, animal, and Earth healing. That avenue, along with the concepts of vibrational medicine and emotional healing, are new, highly important fields for the healing of people and the planet.

The four concepts all go together. No one is healthy who eats chemical laden, genetically manipulated, nutritionally depleted foods. No human or animal is healthy on chemical prescription drugs that suppress symptoms without addressing the causes of dis-ease. Health that addresses only the physical body, denying the emotions and emotional healing, is not health at all. And people (and animals) cannot heal on an unhealthy planet, so that healing always involves both Earth and her inhabitants. Plants are directly necessary for life on this planet. Flowers have a part to play that has barely been explored until now, or has been long forgotten. Their beauty is an invitation to look closer and remember, and to learn once more from Goddess Earth. The following pages are a beginning of that remembering.

What Are Flower Essences?

Flowers are the reproductive organs of the plants that sustain life on Goddess Earth. They are the purest development of the life essence of the plant, and the plant's highest vibrational energy, as well as that of the planet. Flower energy is highly refined and purified. It partakes of all the four levels of Be-ing (physical, emotional, mental, and spiritual). The vibrational level of flowers is faster and more refined than the vibrational level of human energy, and therefore has the ability to aid and heal human or animal energy vibrations. Each plant species, and each individual person, has a unique vibrational rate. When a flower's rate of vibration matches something missing in human energy, the plant can work to replace the energy that is needed. Flowers also work to align and balance human energy on a vibrational and emotional level.

All life is vibrational. Life in plants, animals, insects, birds, and people culminates in the physical body but does not begin there, and in fact is comprised of several levels. While the physical body is the most obvious, there are four other bodies that directly comprise it. These bodies are the etheric double, the emotional, mental, and spiritual levels.

The etheric double is an energy twin of the physical body; both dis-ease and wellness manifest there before they reach the physical level, and physical dis-ease can be healed there. The emotional body is the bridge between body and mind, the physical and mental levels. Today's healing is primarily from this level, as people reawaken to emotion and feeling and to clearing the hurts of our pasts and past lives. Flower essences primarily work on this level, and also on the mental and spiritual levels. The mental body is the all-creative mind: we are what we think. Thoughts of pain and limitation restrict our growth, while those of freedom make us whole. The spiritual body is who we are in relation to the Goddess and the universe; we all have a place and value in the Goddess' plan.

These four levels are the nearest to the physical body, and their electrical energy creates it. They are not all we are by any means. (More detailed descriptions of life energy and structure are given in later chapters.) For the moment, it is enough to state that all life is vibrational and begins with the four vibrational bodies. The highly refined electrical vibrations of flowers aid human and animal healing through these four bodies, entering the physical body through the central nervous system. Flowers rebalance human energy that has become erratic or overloaded by stress, painful emotions, rapid change, negative thoughtforms, illness, or through physical, emotional, or mental exhaustion. They aid in the synchronization and alignment of the four vibrational bodies and beyond, of the chakra energy centers on those bodies, and in the balance and alignment of the energies at each level. They also aid in developing the spiritual body, by fostering Goddess within consciousness of oneself as a spiritual Be-ing.

Electrical misalignment, misfiring, and imbalance occur primarily due to stress, which is emotional and mental, and is the cause of 85% or more of human dis-ease. By using flower essences to correct the negative effects of stress, dis-ease in the body is prevented or lessened and emotional balance is regained. Flowers vibrate at a refined level as part of the highest essence of Goddess and the planet. When used as essences, flowers transmit refined Goddess vibration and affect the physical and vibrational bodies of the person who takes them. Flower essences bring spirit into form, Goddess into the human or animal body. Their higher level vibrations raise the energy vibrations of those who use them, resulting in peace, comfort, and well-being.

People have always appreciated flowers and used them as healers. They are expressions of friendship and love when given as gifts, are used to comfort the sick and bereaved, and are symbols of joy and fidelity at weddings. They always bring smiles and delight. In Victorian England, though probably the idea originated in Japan and China, each flower type had a specific meaning, and bouquets were sent, usually in courtship, that were living messages. Essential flower oils (not flower essences) have potent healing properties and stimulate physiological changes and effects. Lavender oil is an all-healer, while tea tree oil is a general antiseptic and immune builder. Witches recognize magickal uses for many flowers and plants; they use cedar or sage for purification and yarrow for protection. Children pick the petals from daisies saying, "She loves me, she loves me not," and hold buttercups to each other's throats to "see if she loves butter." There are flowers for each birth sign and birth date, and flowers have been used as symbols and oracles, omens and traditions throughout Earth's herstory.[1]

Flowers are also living things, with living presences. They have consciousness that can be contacted and much to teach us. Flower essences created in cooperation with the plant's living presence become highly potent healers. Plants have consciousness and presence, and learning to contact the plant devas and tree dryads opens a new awareness of other worlds on Earth. Flower essences are made in cooperation with this consciousness for the benefit of all. In the process, flower devas and humans learn to work together once more, and the resulting flower essences are made stronger and more focused for healing. The remembering of cooperation between dimensional Be-ings is also another aspect of healing the Earth.

Conscious awareness in plants has been demonstrated scientifically. Polygraph tests by Cleve Backster in the 1960s proved plant awareness and response to human threats, their ability to distinguish the person threatening them from other people, and their ability to respond to threats and danger toward other plants or organisms. Plants have emotions and feelings toward human beings, positive and negative feelings, likes and dislikes. They have emotions and the ability to express them, responding on a psychic level that nearly anyone can be taught to access. Such psychic level communication is used in the making of flower essences and has been a major part of other plant research. Plant developers Gregor Mendel, Luther Burbank, and George Washington Carver openly spoke of contacting the consciousness of the plants they researched. The plants "talked to them," and they were humble enough to listen.[2]

The first flower essences were developed by native women in many lands many centuries ago, notably in China, India, and Australia. The healing wells of Old Europe were potentized as flower essences by putting specific leaves or nuts into them before drinking the waters. These ancient wells were places belonging to Persephone and Brede (Bride, Bridgit), the Maiden Goddesses of the witch-healers. The wells still exist, though most are covered over today. Flower essences were used by Paracelsus in the 1500s, at a time when male doctors learned their trade from the women healers whom they did not credit. The art of potentizing water with flower blossom energy for emotional, mental, and spiritual healing is not new.

Modern knowledge and revival of flower essences was begun through work in the 1930s by an English homeopathic doctor, Edward Bach (1886–1936). Disillusioned with the harm done by medicine, he sought gentler methods. As a homeopath, his focus on plant vibrations was understandable. Bach was highly sensitive, able to channel information on the flowers by placing them in his mouth and experiencing their effects on his emotions, mind, and body. He discovered that certain wildflower blossoms placed in pure water, picked and prepared in full bloom on clear sunny days, could be used to heal negative emotional states. Bach understood that emotional pain (defined as worry, stress, anxiety, fear, negative thoughts, and poor self-confidence) is the source of most or all physical dis-ease. He developed thirty-eight remedies to alleviate these states, and tested these remedies on people and pets. After his death, this research has continued.[3] His work was the beginning of modern flower essence knowledge. Today there are other flower essence sources in several countries.

While many flower essences are available today commercially prepared, I believe it is important to teach people to make their own. The process is simple and inexpensive. People are drawn directly to the plant or plants that have the healing properties they need. Flowers that one can see, touch, and experience make far more effective healers than those known only from descriptions on a bottle or in a book.

Flowers are available everywhere. Developing the psychic contact with plant devas is not difficult, and the relationship with devas, dryads, and nature spirits is a significant part of the healing. So is the empowerment that comes from making your own essences. Gemstones can be added to the flowers in flower essence preparation, enhancing and strengthening their healing effects.

Information follows on how to make and use flower essences and essences combining flowers and gemstones for personal healing at home.

How to Make Flower Essences

Flower essences are Earth, air, fire, and water combined. They are made from the blossoms of plants, which have required water, sun, soil, and carbon dioxide to grow. The flowers are placed in a clear bowl of pure water on the Earth, where the sun and air imprint the plant essence into the water. Plant devas, nature spirits of the angelic realm who have shaped and directed the Goddess life force energy into the plant and flower form, then copy that form and pattern into the flower essence. The magick of flower essence creation is just a small mirroring of the magickal growth of the flowers.

A flower essence is easily made and requires just a few household tools. You will need a clear glass bowl without design or pattern on it, scissors, a glass cup, a funnel, brown (or other light-proof) glass storage bottles, a preserving medium (usually brandy), and labels for the bottles. To use the finished essence, you will need two brown glass eyedropper bottles with glass droppers. All tools must be scrupulously clean, though boiling them is unnecessary, and it is best if flower essence tools and bottles have not been used for other purposes. If you choose to combine flowers and gemstones in your essences, you will need a selection of crystals and colored gemstones. Before using them, these must be washed and their energy cleared.

Bowls and storage bottles must be glass; plastics or metals flake off into the water. The bowl must be clear, as colors and designs also effect the energy and imprinting of the essence. Large clear salad bowls are easily available and inexpensive in supermarkets or houseware stores. Storage bottles and eye-dropper bottles are of colored glass—brown, blue, or green—to make them light proof, preventing deterioration of the finished flower essence. Small brown eyedropper bottles (half ounce, one ounce, or two ounce size) are available from health food stores, herb stores, and some drugstores. They are becoming harder to find in glass since many stores are changing to plastic bottles. Large storage bottles for the finished tinctures are most easily found in the supermarket. For the easiest and cheapest source, buy brown glass prune juice bottles and wash them thoroughly.

One other item is required—a preserving medium for the finished essence, both in the storage and eyedropper bottles. Without this preserving medium, the essence will deteriorate and sour quickly, probably overnight or sooner. The traditional flower essence preservative has been brandy, which is used to fill a third to half of each storage bottle and about a third of the dropper bottles. This is the most stable medium available and is recommended for at least the storage bottles if you plan on keeping your essences permanently or for a long time. In the dropper bottles, however, for those sensitive to alcohol there are two other options. One is white vinegar (apple cider vinegar tastes better but preserves less well), and the other is a strong tea of the herb plant red shiso, also called perilla. This last medium has been researched by Molly Sheehan of Green Hope Farm and is available from her. Only a few drops of essence from the storage bottle go into the first eyedropper bottle, and only a few drops from the first eyedropper bottle go into the second bottle to be taken internally, so very little brandy is actually consumed. The bottles and preserving medium are the two items in flower essence production that involve some expense, and that also may not be readily at hand.

In keeping with Goddess tradition, the most potent flower essences are made in accordance with sun and moon cycles. Make them in the waxing/increasing time of the year and in the waxing/increasing time of the moon. This means that essences are the strongest when made in spring or summer and on New to Full Moon days. Even though I live in Florida where flowers bloom all year round and warm temperatures prevail, my guides have permitted me to make essences only from Candlemas (February 1) to Hallows (October 31). The barren time of year, from Hallows to Candlemas, is not the time to make healing essences. Likewise, my essences are made on the Full Moon, if possible, or close to that time. I am permitted to make essences from the first day of the moon cycle (New Moon) until a few days after the Full Moon (fourteenth day of the cycle). The time of the Waning Moon, the last ten days or so of the lunar month, are also barren times and usually not positive for essence making. There have been some exceptions, but this is the rule.

To begin the process, on a bright sunny day, choose the dayblooming flowers to become your essence. Nightblooming plants are best made into essences at night on Full Moons. Information is given later on how to determine what a flower or flower-gem combination does in healing. Assume you have decided what flower (or flower and gems) will become your essence, that the blooming plant is available to you, and that you have assembled the tools to make the essence. Start as early in the day as possible, noon at the latest, and begin by filling your clear bowl with pure water. Filtered, bottled, or spring water are fine. Do not use tap water. Distilled water is also not recommended, as all life has been removed from it. The water should not be carbonated. Do not touch the water or the inside of the bowl.

Take the bowl and clean scissors into the garden and place the bowl of water at the foot of the plant on the dirt, not on concrete. Put the scissors down, and sit or stand in front of the plant. Briefly enter a light meditative state. Focus on the plant and its flowers. Admire the flowers for their beauty as a part of Goddess Earth. Do this silently, in your mind, rather than speaking aloud. Stop and listen for a moment—there may be some response; you will hear or feel it in your mind subtly and gently. Next, ask to speak with the deva or life force of the plant. Ask if the plant is willing for you to take a few (never all) of its flowers for use in a healing flower essence. Tell the plant you will appreciate its gift and honor it. Again wait for some response, which again will be quiet and subtle.

If the response is favorable (you will know when it is not), pick up your scissors and ask the plant and plant deva which flowers are willing to be part of your essence. Pause before each blossom, and if you perceive a yes, you may cut the flower. Do not touch the flower with your hands, but hold the bowl under it and let the flower drop into the bowl. Unlike some flower essence makers, I use whole flowers left intact, sometimes with an occasional leaf attached. One flower may be enough to make an essence, but if there is an abundance, take enough flowers to cover the top surface of the water in the bowl. Take only flowers that are unblemished and that the plant agrees to offer. Say thanks. An offering to the plant of a pinch of cornmeal or a bit of organic tobacco is usually appreciated.

When the flowers are in the water, place the bowl again at the base of the plant, or as near to it as possible in full sunlight. Ask the deva of the plant to help you in making your essence and, if you are a Reiki practitioner, trace the Reiki symbols over the bowl, water, and blossoms. If you wish to use gemstones in the essence, add them before you fill the bowl with water. Thank the plant and plant deva again and leave the bowl to infuse in the sun for about three hours, longer if the day is not fully sunny. Essences made in moonlight also take three hours. If you have pets that use the yard where the essence is being made, keep them indoors or keep an eye on them. Dogs are attracted to the energy and may drink from the bowl, urinate on it, or take the flowers out as playthings if they are not prevented from doing so. Birds, cats, or wild animals may drink from the bowl but will do less harm.

At the end of three hours, repeat the Reiki symbols and bring the bowl into the house. Again, do not touch the water. Place the bowl in the kitchen sink, the easiest place to work. Fill your storage bottles a third to half full of brandy. Using a cup to dip with and a funnel, fill the remainder of the bottles with the flower essence water. Do not put plant matter or gemstones into the storage bottles; fill them through a sieve if necessary. Always label the bottles, including the date made and the flowers and gemstones that are in the essence. This is your Mother Tincture, and if capped tightly and preserved with brandy, it will keep permanently. Return the leftover water and used flowers to the Earth at the base of the plant.

Next, fill a small eyedropper bottle about a third of the way with preservative (brandy, white vinegar, or red shiso). For a half-ounce bottle, add five drops of Mother Tincture; add seven drops for a one-ounce bottle, or nine drops for a two-ounce bottle. Fill the rest of the bottle with pure water. This is your stock bottle. When you buy flower essences from a supplier, this is what you receive. You may take your essences directly from the stock bottle, or further dilute it one more time. To make a dosage bottle, take the other small eye-dropper bottle and fill it a third full of preserving medium. Add ten drops from the stock bottle and fill the rest of the way with pure water. You may add drops from more than one flower essence stock bottle to your dosage bottle to take several essences at once. It is usually best not to take more than four essences together at a time this way . To use the essences, take four drops from the dosage bottle on or under your tongue two or three times a day.

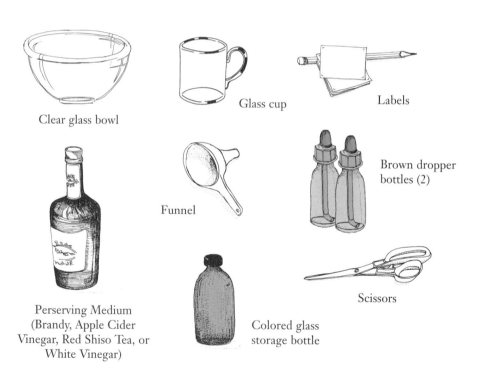

Clear glass bowl

Glass cup

Labels

Funnel

Brown dropper bottles (2)

Perserving Medium
(Brandy, Apple Cider
Vinegar, Red Shiso Tea, or
White Vinegar)

Colored glass
storage bottle

Scissors

Which Essences Should I Take?

The most commonly asked question about flower essences is, "How do I know which flower essence/s to take?" Commercial flower essence companies offer hundreds of choices, and their bottles of essences usually come in sets of nine or more. Once you begin making your own, you will also have a variety to choose from. Once you choose your essence or essences, how long should you take it, and how do you know when you no longer need it? An essence that seems right on one day may not seem so the next. If you plan to make your own, how do you know which flowers to make into essences? If you wish to add crystals and gems to your essences, how do you know what to add?

Starting with a set of ready-made essences in stock bottles, first look at the usage key given by the company. What appeals to you or seems to be what you need? The key is only a guideline, however, and probably the least useful guide to individual requirements. Next, handle each bottle one at a time, entering a light meditative state to do so, asking your spirit guides to help. If you are sensitive, the bottles containing energies you need will have a special feel. They may seem to tingle, feel cold or hot; you may psychically see light or bright colors, or hear a "yes" when touching them. Set those bottles aside, then look at their meanings on the usage key. There may be one, two, or several from the set. Take a drop of each essence under your tongue, one at a time, pausing still in the meditative state to notice impressions. An essence that offers something you need will feel very good. It will calm you, make you feel joyful, or make you feel filled with light. These are the essences you need today and will probably respond to for at least a couple of weeks.

Make your dosage bottle from these essences, but it is best to limit the number in the dosage bottle to four different flower essences or less. If you have responded to more essences, take the bottles from the box and set them together. Ask inwardly to be shown the combination that is good for you. Then set aside one bottle at a time and see how the remaining combination feels. If it still feels good without a particular essence, eliminate that bottle for now. If it does not, return that bottle and try with the others. If it seems that none of them can be removed from the combination, use them all, but remember, combinations are the most effective with four or fewer energies. Again, use the meditative state and ask your spirit guides to help. Use the agreed upon combination for two weeks before testing again.

Another way to choose, perhaps a simpler one, is to use a pendulum. This can be any small object dangling from a string, a crystal on a silver chain, or even a pendant necklace you've been wearing. Make sure the energy in your chosen pendulum is fully cleared before depending on it for answers to your flower essence questions. Clearing can be done by smudging the pendulum with sage smoke, burying it in dry sea salt overnight, soaking it in sea salt and water, or leaving it under a pyramid overnight. Ask that your spirit guides or other high level Be-ings run the pendulum for you, for optimal accuracy. Ask also that only high level energy from the Goddess enter this divination tool.

To learn to use a pendulum, first dangle it freely from your dominant hand (right if you are right-handed), holding the string at the top with your thumb and first two fingers. Focus your mind upon it and ask your guides to show you a "yes" response. The pendulum (weight at the bottom) will begin to swing, and the pattern it swings in is an indication of "yes." Then focus again and ask to see a "no"—the swing will look different. Yes and no responses in pendulums are often individual; a "yes" to one person may not mean "yes" to another. Get used to the pendulum's responses by asking some evident questions, all with yes and no answers. "Is my name Jane?" "Do I live in a house?" etc.

When you are confident, begin asking questions you don't know the answers to, ones in which you have no emotional investment. Ask questions that really don't matter. For questions in which you *do* have emotional investment, you must learn to keep your mind neutral in the asking or the pendulum will simply tell you what you wish to hear. Once you are used to the working of the pendulum and confident that your spirit guides are willing to work with the pendulum, begin to use it as a healing tool. It can be very accurate in helping you choose your flower essences (and any number of other things) and in eliminating less useful essences from a combination. Hold the essence bottles in your hand, one at a time, and ask if this essence is good for you at this time. If you wish to use it for *choosing essences* for someone else or a pet, focus on the other person or pet while running the pendulum and holding each essence bottle. Use the meditative state and connect with your spirit guides as much as possible while doing this.

Another way to test for flower essences is by applied kinesiology muscle testing, using your body as a pendulum. There are several ways to use this method. In the simplest, stand and hold the bottle of flower essence against your heart chakra (center chest). Close your eyes and allow your body to sway freely. If you feel yourself swaying backwards, the essence is not positive for you—the answer is "no." If you sway forward, the essence is right for you at this time—the answer is "yes." Remember to keep your eyes closed and your body relaxed while testing .

Another kinesiology method involves using your fingers and is the preferred method of Machaelle Small Wright of Perelandra Flower Essences. If you are right-handed, hold your left palm up and connect the tip of your left thumb with the tip of your left little finger. Place the thumb and *index* finger of your right hand inside the finger circle of the left hand. Hold the left hand circle tight. Ask a question with a yes or no answer, then gently press the inside (right-hand) fingers against the left-hand finger circle. If the answer is "yes," the left-hand fingers will not pull apart easily; if the answer is "no," they will separate without much pressure. If you are left-handed, reverse the hands. This method can be used for any yes or no questions, not only in choosing flower essences.

Diagram 1.
Kinesiology Self-Testing Steps[4]

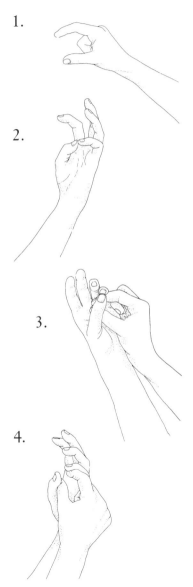

1.

2.

3.

4.

1. The circuit fingers: if you are right handed: place your left hand palm up. Connect the tip of your left thumb with the tip of the left little finger (not your index finger). If you are left-handed: place your right hand palm up. Connect the tip of your right thumb with the tip of your right little finger....

2. The test fingers: to test the circuit . . . place the thumb and index finger of your other hand inside the circle you have created by connecting your thumb and little finger. The thumb/index finger should be right under the thumb/little finger, touching them. Don't try to make a circle with your test fingers . . . .It will look as if the circuit fingers are resting on the test fingers.

3. Keeping this position, ask yourself a yes/no question in which you already know the answer to be yes . . . .Once you've asked the question, press your circuit fingers together, keeping the tip-to-tip position. Using the same amount of pressure, try to pull apart the circuit fingers with your test fingers. Press the lower thumb against the upper thumb, the lower index finger against the upper little finger....

If the answer to the question is positive . . ., you will not be able to easily pull apart the circuit fingers....Important: Be sure the amount of pressure holding together the circuit fingers is equal to the amount pressing against them with your testing fingers. Also, don't use a pumping action in your testing fingers when trying to pry your circuit fingers apart. Use an equal, steady, and continuous pressure....

4. Once you have a clear sense of the positive response, ask yourself a question that has a negative answer. Again press your circuit fingers together and, using equal pressure, press against the circuit fingers with the test fingers. This time the electrical circuit will break and the circuit fingers will weaken and separate....

The traditional method of kinesiology testing requires two participants. The person who wants the information holds the bottle of flower essence to be tested in either hand and holds her opposite arm straight out. The second person then asks, "Is this essence good for her at this time?" and presses gently on the first person's outstretched arm at the wrist. If the answer is "yes" the first person's arm remains steady; if the answer is "no" minimal pressure will cause her arm to fall. Only light steady pressure on the wrist is needed, not strong force.

To use this method to test for a pet or a child, the first person touches the pet with the same hand that holds the flower essence. She extends her other arm, and the second person presses on the outstretched wrist asking, "Is this essence good for the dog or child at this time?" Again, if the first person's arm remains steady, the answer is "yes"; if her arm falls easily, it's a "no." This method is called surrogate muscle testing. When using any form of muscle testing or pendulum work, it is important to remain focused on the question at hand. Ask only yes or no questions phrased in the most direct, simple way.

Diagram 2.
Muscle Testing

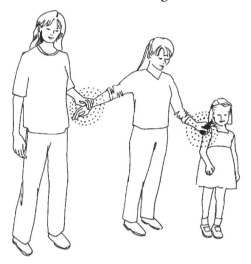

Surrogate Testing for Another Person

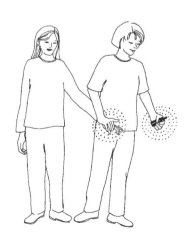

Surrogate Testing for a Pet   **Muscle Testing for Yourself**

Any of the methods described will help you choose which flower essence/s are right for you at any given time. Developing the sensitivity to do it by simple touch is the most optimal and ultimately the most accurate method.

Finding the Meanings of Flowers and Gemstones

The methods in the previous chapter can help you to choose which flower essences are positive for you at a specific time. But how would you determine which growing flowers to make into your own essences? And if you wish to add gemstones to your essences, which stones are positive with which flowers? Finding answers to these questions has been uncharted ground for the most part. I have made flower essences from Florida flowers for the last three years and I include gemstones with each. I choose the flowers and gemstones by channeling in a very simple way.

You will need a lined notebook and pen, and possibly a chair to sit on outdoors. When I first began doing this work, I needed to see the living plant and touch the flower to determine its uses. After a while, I could do this by memory—with plants and flowers I had seen recently and was familiar with but not actually in physical contact with. Later on, I became able to channel meanings for flowers from garden catalogs, though it still requires clear photographs in color. Black and white photos or sketches of plants won't work. In channeling gemstone meanings, it is usually necessary to see and touch the stones.

Go to the blooming plant you wish to find meanings for and sit quietly beside it with your notebook. Touch the flower with your left hand, without picking it. Enter the meditative state and ask to be in contact with the life force energy or deva of the plant. Ask the deva to honor you by telling you the healing uses of her plant as a flower essence. Write down the information that comes into your mind. Do this quickly and immediately as you receive it, or the information will likely be lost. Write exactly what you perceive without judgment or analysis. When you feel you have received all the information, thank the deva and stop touching the flower. Go to the next plant that you wish information about. You may do several of these in a row, but you will find yourself becoming surprisingly tired very quickly. Do only a few per day and don't do this work every day.

To determine the meanings of healing gemstones, work in the same manner. Stones also have life force energy and devas that are usually willing to tell you what their gems and minerals can do as healers. Your own spirit guides will aid the contact with plant or gemstone devas if you ask them to, or the guides may also give you the information themselves. Again, have your notebook handy. Hold the stone in one hand while writing with the other. Do not depend on your memory—it will fail you—write the meanings down. Write exactly what you hear or perceive, without judgment.

Two aspects of flower and gemstone energy will help you greatly in finding their meanings as healers. These lie in the form and the color of the plant or stone. What a plant or stone resembles, or its name resembles, may be what it heals or can be used for. A flower shaped like a trumpet may assist psychic hearing, for example, as does the King's Mantle flower in my Channeling Essence II (see Flower Combinations). Impatiens, one of the Bach Flower Remedies, is used to calm impatient and irritable people, as the plant name suggests. Angel Trumpet flowers (see Channeling Essence I, Old Soul Essence, and Star Woman Essence) assist angelic contact and psychic communication with angels, as do the gemstones Angelite or Angel Wing Selenite.

In the case of flowering herbs or vegetables, be aware also of what the herb or vegetable does nutritionally, medicinally, or traditionally. Corn, for example, is honored by Native American people for its sustenance in spiritual and physical ways. As a flower essence, corn is used for grounding and for being present in the body while at the same time respecting and partaking of spiritual energy. The corn flower is used as an essence for those who spend too much time out of body, and who may not be nourishing their physical bodies or physical lives properly. Yarrow, a healing herb for fever, physical cleansing, and blood sugar balancing has been used tradition-ally by witches in the home as a protection against negative energy. Yarrow flower essence (Protection Essence I and II, Astral Essence, and Shield Essence) is an energy protector and balancer. The concept is useful with gemstones, too. Onyx, which is traditionally used for mourning, in an essence aids in completing the grieving process and in understanding that life is eternal.

A plant or gemstone's color is also a major clue, based on the colors found in human and animal energy, especially the colors of the chakras. There are seven major energy centers called chakras on the human etheric double level and another thirteen on the emotional body aura. Each chakra matches a specific part of the body and has designated emotional and physical coordinates. A flower or gemstone in a chakra-matching color gives indication by its color of what it does or heals. Light blue, for example, is the color of the etheric double throat chakra, and blue stones or flowers often heal the throat or throat center issues. These issues can include the ability to speak out or speak one's needs, to understand and express one's feelings or truth, to stimulate creativity, to aid psychic communication, and to enhance the ability to release anger safely.

The thirteen energy centers on the emotional body, the hara line newly developing in many people, usually have meanings concerning one's purpose for incarnating in this lifetime. Orange-gold flowers and stones align and balance the hara chakra. They help the individual to understand, develop, and manifest her life purpose and bring it into its earthplane expression. The transpersonal point chakra just above the crown of the head fosters awareness of spirituality and connection with the Goddess. White flowers and white or clear gemstones open, clear, align, and develop that chakra and the person's spirituality. Detailed analysis of the etheric double and hara line chakras are given in the next two sections. For information on the chakras in pets, see my book *Natural Healing for Dogs and Cats* (The Crossing Press, 1993). With the chakra information that follows, colors' meaning in flowers and gemstones becomes more clear. Detailed gemstone information is also available in my book *Healing with Gemstones and Crystals* (The Crossing Press, 1996).

By observing the color of a flower that you wish to make an essence from, you are immediately given information as to what chakra it serves. When you understand the color in terms of what that chakra does in human or animal energy, you already have a great deal of information on what that flower in an essence will do. When you add to that flower the gemstones that do similar things, have similar colors and similar uses, the stones focus and intensify the flower essence's use and energy. Combine that information with your observations on the name of the plant, what it looks like or resembles and its traditions, and you probably have the use of that plant and gemstone combination as a flower essence. Choose the gemstones you wish to include by pendulum or muscle testing. Sit down with your notebook, tune into the plant's devic presence, and write down the information you are given. The pieces of the puzzle come together, and the uses for that flower and gemstone essence become clear. Make the essence with confidence of its purpose.

When adding gemstones to flower essences, it is important to note that the stones must be fully energy cleared and cleansed before using them. This is absolutely essential. Clear gemstones by the methods described in Chapter 4 for clearing pendulums. Stones that are not energy cleared can disrupt the purpose of a flower essence and of any other use they are put to. An uncleared pendulum has no accuracy and may give wildly erratic responses.

In another gemstone note, I always add Danburite and either Clear Quartz Crystal or Herkimer Diamond to the other stones in my essences. Danburite is an energy softener, purifier, and enhancer of other stones and of flower essence energy. Clear Quartz Crystal and Herkimer Diamonds are magnifiers; they intensify the effects of the essence and bring light into the person's aura as she uses that essence combination.

I have tested my essences on a variety of people who have tried them. Some have been given an essence without explanation; they simply were asked to try it and to tell me what it seemed to do. I have told others about the meanings that I've derived from the flowers and gemstones and asked them to verify if they worked the same way for them. Occasionally someone adds to my definitions and meanings, but so far no one has told me that an essence does something very differently from what I've designated for it. This is true whether the person knows my channelled meanings beforehand or not. My essences have been tested on animals, as well. The method of obtaining flower and gemstone information works—it is simpler than it sounds. It may take some practice to become expert at this method, but anyone can use it to make their own effective flower, or flower and gemstone, essences.

The Kundalini Chakras

Since flower essences primarily affect the nonphysical bodies and flower and gemstone colors match the chakras, some understanding of soul structure is important to flower essence users and makers. The kundalini chakras are located on the etheric double aura level, also known as the physical body aura. The etheric double is the closest energy layer to the dense physical body and considered to be its mirror twin. Dis-ease will manifest in the etheric double before it reaches the physical body. Dis-ease can also be healed and removed from the body at that place. The kundalini central channel, called the Sushumna, runs vertically up and down the center of the human body at the etheric double level. Beside and criss-crossing the central channel are two smaller channels, the Ida and Pingala. These begin at the root center (at the tailbone), and end at the left and right nostril. The seven chakras with body correspondences are located on the Sushumna in the loops between where Ida and Pingala cross. The energy movement of the two winding channels is reminiscent of the shape of our current two-strand DNA molecule. Energy rises through the kundalini chakras along these channels.

In ancient and modern traditions, spiritual development has always begun with bringing energy through the kundalini channels to open, develop, and clear the chakras. This discipline is the source of yoga, meditation, and of most psychic opening work. As the chakras fill with energy, they are cleared of obstructions and healed, bringing increased physical health and psychic growth. Energy moves upward through the chakras, the seven energy centers, from the root to the crown, the physical to spiritual levels. Each ascending chakra measures development in human growth, as well as coordinates to and reflects physical anatomy and health. Each chakra also connects to a level of the four aura bodies.

The first three chakras—the root (red), belly (orange), and solar plexus (yellow)—are linked to physical body survival. The root connects to the etheric double-physical body aura layer. The belly chakra accesses the emotional body on its closest-to-physical level, and the solar plexus links to the lower level of the mental body, the conscious rational mind. The next three—the heart (green/pink), throat (light blue), and brow (indigo)—define the higher human needs of the intuitive mind and basic spirituality. They are the first entrances into the outer aura bodies.

The heart center is the higher mental body level, the intuitive creative mind. It offers access to the astral body twin and the astral plane (through the hara line thymus chakra just above it). The throat chakra is the seat of communication on many levels, and also accesses the Etheric template level, which is the physical body's blueprint. The throat is the first level of the spiritual body. The brow chakra, second spiritual body layer, is the human psychic center. Its access to the outer levels is the Celestial body, the template for the emotional self.

The seventh center, the crown (violet), is purely spiritual, the highest of the three spiritual levels of the four bodies. Its outer body connection is to access the Ketheric body, the blueprint for the mental body, Light Body, and the mental grids.

The above are the outer body extensions of the seven major chakras and the four bodies (physical, emotional, mental, and spiritual). This may be new information for many healers, but most people have knowledge of the kundalini chakras themselves, without their aura body access links. In the past, most or all flower essence and gemstone healing was based on simply balancing and clearing the kundalini chakras. I will list them as simply and briefly as possible below. Pay particular attention to their colors, as they match the colors of the flowers and gemstones for each center.

The chakras begin at the base of the spine and finish at the top of the head. Though fixed in the central spinal column (the Sushumna), they are located on both the front and back of the body, and work through it. The first center is the *root chakra*, represented by the color *red*, and located at the tailbone or coccyx in back and pubic bone at the body's front. This center holds the basic needs of survival, security, and safety, and the ability to be grounded into earthplane existence in the body.[7] In the body, root anatomy include the hips, legs, lower back, rectum, vagina, and uterus. The root chakra connects to the etheric double aura, and red flowers and gemstones heal and balance it.

Next is the *belly chakra*, located between the pubic bone and the navel, and also rooted in the spine. *Orange* is the color for this center and orange flowers and stones, and its basic needs are for sexuality, self-esteem as personal power, and power in the world. This center accesses the lowest level of the emotional body and houses one's unhealed inner child. Images of

Diagram 3.
The Twelve Chakras of Barbara Marciniak[5]

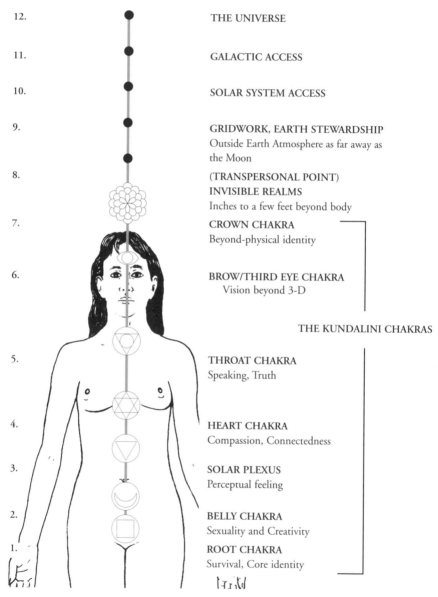

12.   THE UNIVERSE

11.   GALACTIC ACCESS

10.   SOLAR SYSTEM ACCESS

9.   GRIDWORK, EARTH STEWARDSHIP
Outside Earth Atmosphere as far away as the Moon

8.   (TRANSPERSONAL POINT)
INVISIBLE REALMS
Inches to a few feet beyond body

7.   CROWN CHAKRA
Beyond-physical identity

6.   BROW/THIRD EYE CHAKRA
Vision beyond 3-D

THE KUNDALINI CHAKRAS

5.   THROAT CHAKRA
Speaking, Truth

4.   HEART CHAKRA
Compassion, Connectedness

3.   SOLAR PLEXUS
Perceptual feeling

2.   BELLY CHAKRA
Sexuality and Creativity

1.   ROOT CHAKRA
Survival, Core identity

Diagram 4.
The Aura Body Levels[6]

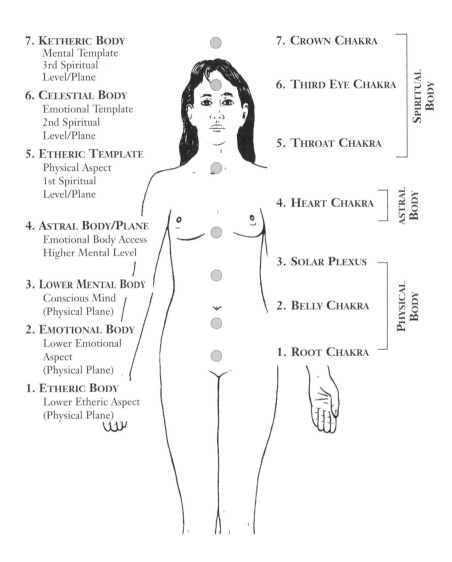

7. KETHERIC BODY
Mental Template
3rd Spiritual
Level/Plane

6. CELESTIAL BODY
Emotional Template
2nd Spiritual
Level/Plane

5. ETHERIC TEMPLATE
Physical Aspect
1st Spiritual
Level/Plane

4. ASTRAL BODY/PLANE
Emotional Body Access
Higher Mental Level

3. LOWER MENTAL BODY
Conscious Mind
(Physical Plane)

2. EMOTIONAL BODY
Lower Emotional
Aspect
(Physical Plane)

1. ETHERIC BODY
Lower Etheric Aspect
(Physical Plane)

7. CROWN CHAKRA

6. THIRD EYE CHAKRA

5. THROAT CHAKRA

SPIRITUAL BODY

4. HEART CHAKRA

ASTRAL BODY

3. SOLAR PLEXUS

2. BELLY CHAKRA

1. ROOT CHAKRA

PHYSICAL BODY

both this life and past life traumas are stored here, and the ability to let go of old emotions is based at this chakra. Belly chakra body parts include the ovaries, uterus, fallopian tubes, pelvis, lumbar spine, kidneys, bladder, and large intestine.

The *solar plexus* is the third chakra, located at the level of the lowest ribs. Its color is *yellow*, and the center is the body's receiver, distributor, and processor of energy and perceptual feeling. It is the lower layer of the mental body, representing the conscious and rational mind. Self-confidence and survival intuition, business and math sense, and material-level learning ability are focused here, as well as self-empowerment and the will. Body parts for this chakra include the stomach, liver, gall bladder, pancreas, and small intestine.

The second mental body chakra, the center of the creative and intuitive mind, is located at the *heart*. This chakra connects body and mind with spirit and is located behind the breast bone between the breasts in front and on the spine between the shoulder blades in back. The heart chakra directs one's ability to love oneself and others, to give and to receive. Two colors represent this center, *pink* and *green*, and pink is the primary flower color for essences. Almost everyone in modern culture seems to have a hard, hurt, or broken heart, and it is no accident that heart dis-ease is the number one killer in America. Deep heart hurts can result in aura obstructions called heart scars. When these release, they raise quantities of old pain, but free the heart for softening, healing, and new growth. Organs for this center include the heart, lungs, circulatory system, shoulders, and the upper back.

The final three chakras comprise the spiritual body aura, the throat, brow, and crown centers. The *throat chakra*, located in the V of the collar bone at the lower neck, is represented by the color *light blue* and by light blue flowers and healing stones. This is women's center of communication, expression, hearing (including psychic hearing), receiving others, and creativity. It contains and is access to the Etheric template, the blueprint of the physical body. This is possibly the most complex of the chakras, as every possibility for change, transformation, and healing are located here, including that of healing one's future via the past through karmic release. The throat is where anger is stored and finally let go of. Body parts for this center include the throat, neck, jaw and teeth, ears and hearing, and the thyroid gland.

The *indigo* sixth chakra, located above the eyes on the center of the forehead, is called the *brow chakra* or third eye. This is the place of seeing beyond physical realities into the psychic realm for an understanding of nonphysical truth. The chakra is the second spiritual aura body layer and contains access to the Celestial body template. I define this center as the place of Goddess within or the Buddhist Nonvoid, and the crown chakra as Goddess herself or the Void. Physical body parts for this center include the eyes, face, brain, lymphatic, and endocrine systems. Darker blue flowers and indigo gemstones match this chakra.

The *crown* is the seventh kundalini chakra, located just behind the top of the skull. Its color is described as *violet*, or white with a golden core, and it is the third spiritual body level with access to the Ketheric template. The center is women's connection with Goddess and the Void, the place where life animates the physical body. The silver cord that connects the aura bodies extends from the crown, and the crown's continuation leads outward from the spiritual body to the outer bodies, the Body of Light, and the oversoul. The soul comes into the body at birth through the crown and leaves from the crown at death. This is the seat of awareness of having a beyond-physical identity and a part in the universal Goddess plan. Physical body parts for the crown chakra include the central nervous system and the spine.

In one further comment on the kundalini line, Barbara Marciniak describes the development of five new centers beyond the crown. This eventual total of twelve chakras will match the future reconnection of the twelve DNA strands. The centers continue along the straight central line of the Sushumna, reaching from the individual to the universe. They are beyond the body and have no physical coordinates, but a few flower essences and gemstones access them. Her eighth chakra accesses invisible psychic realities beyond the body; the center is located just above the crown from a few inches to a few feet over the head. Chakra nine, located as far outside Earth's atmosphere as the moon, connects the individual to the energy grid of the Earth making one a caretaker and steward for the planet. The tenth center offers access to all the information of Earth's solar system; the eleventh to Earth's galaxy; and the twelfth chakra gives access to the rest of the planets, with information on deep space and the universe.[8] By the future development of these centers, we will truly become the interplanetary Be-ings we were meant to be.

The Hara Line

Energy channels and chakra systems similar to the etheric double kundalini line exist on the other aura body levels. Until recently, most healers have not had access to nor awareness of these other systems. Some people have now begun to notice the opening of new chakras, however, and are gaining awareness of another chakra series. I have named this astral/emotional body energy system the hara line, from Barbara Brennan's description of a three-chakra "Haric Level."[9] Her line and three centers match my perception, but I see a far more developed system of thirteen chakras. A major strength of flower and gemstone essences is their ability to reach and heal this line of chakras, and the emotional body itself.

The hara line holds and maintains our life purpose, why we have incarnated for this lifetime. Clear understanding of this purpose leads to productivity, fulfillment, and peace of mind in one's life. Energy blockage on this emotional body hara level obstructs one's intentions and accomplishments, and the awareness of this purpose. More and more, the emotional body is central to any level of healing, from the physical body to the core soul. As with the kundalini line, the hara chakras have color coordinates that match flowers and gemstones, and access to the chakras and their connecting bodies can be made with essences. The hara level is vitally important for today's healers and healing.

The first hara chakra is a *clear-colored* (all colors, no color) center above the head, which I have called the *transpersonal point*. It is a chakra familiar to many women who have placed it on the kundalini channel. This is the soul's first manifestation into matter, the first opening of energy from the Goddess/Void. It carries the individual's reason to incarnate into her body, mind, emotions, and spirit. The transpersonal point separates and individualizes the soul from its Goddess source, giving the soul a personal reality and a life on Earth. Other names for this center include the Soul Star, and Ch'i Kung calls it the source of Heavenly Ch'i. Some white flowers and clear gemstones activate this center.

Next is a pair of *silver* chakra centers located behind the eyes. I call these *vision chakras*. They can be activated for using the eyes as lasers in healing, as well as for visualization and for manifesting one's needs through visualization. They are considered minor centers but are important for psychic healers. Some of the grey, iridescent, and silvery gemstones combined with white flowers open and develop these chakras.

The *causal body chakra* follows, located in the base of the skull where the neck meets the head at the back. Some healers see this very major center as a light *silvery blue*, while others perceive it as resembling *crimson* yarn wrapped around a golden skein. Flowers and gemstones for this center include both blue and red, with the red more a fuchsia or deep pink. The causal body is described as all potential (the Nonvoid or Goddess within), and the transformer of nonphysical information/light into consciousness, as in channeling, automatic

Diagram 5.
The Hara Line

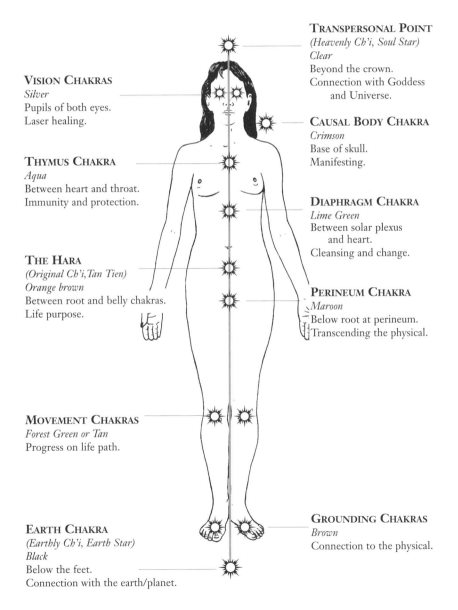

TRANSPERSONAL POINT
(Heavenly Ch'i, Soul Star)
Clear
Beyond the crown.
Connection with Goddess
and Universe.

VISION CHAKRAS
Silver
Pupils of both eyes.
Laser healing.

CAUSAL BODY CHAKRA
Crimson
Base of skull.
Manifesting.

THYMUS CHAKRA
Aqua
Between heart and throat.
Immunity and protection.

DIAPHRAGM CHAKRA
Lime Green
Between solar plexus
and heart.
Cleansing and change.

THE HARA
(Original Ch'i, Tan Tien)
Orange brown
Between root and belly chakras.
Life purpose.

PERINEUM CHAKRA
Maroon
Below root at perineum.
Transcending the physical.

MOVEMENT CHAKRAS
Forest Green or Tan
Progress on life path.

GROUNDING CHAKRAS
Brown
Connection to the physical.

EARTH CHAKRA
(Earthly Ch'i, Earth Star)
Black
Below the feet.
Connection with the earth/planet.

writing, and working with spirit guides. The chakra must be activated and balanced to bring mental commitment to one's life purpose, but this should be done only with all the hara line chakras together. Causal body activation manifests one's spiritual life purpose, as embodied in the entire hara line, into earthplane physical reality.

The next hara line chakra, also a major one, is the *thymus chakra*. I perceive this center's color as *aqua* or aquamarine, and see it as connecting the hara line and emotional body to the kundalini line and etheric double. The center connects a person's emotions to her physical body. On the physical level, this chakra protects the immune system, which is clearly affected by the emotions, and on an emotional level, this chakra contains our wish to live and maintain this incarnation. The center holds our drive and passion to fulfill the task we incarnated to accomplish in this lifetime. It is obviously a vital center, central to most of today's healing issues and dis-ease sources.

You can find the thymus chakra physically. It is located on the chest, between and about three inches above the nipples on the breast bone. When you find it, you will know immediately; it is painful and sensitive to pressure. *Gently* pressing this point "brings oneself whole heartedly awake to the grief we have carried for so long and the vastness which awaits a merciful awareness."[10] Meditating on the sensations that come while touching this point opens and releases grief (which may include anger, resentment, fear, or other feelings). Some white and a few blue flowers with aqua gemstones also activate this center, and much healing happens along the way.

Next below the thymus is the *diaphragm chakra*, at the level of the physical diaphragm muscle, just below the solar plexus. Its color is *lime green*, and it is activated by a few yellow flowers with green or yellow-green gemstones. I perceive this center as providing a clearing and detoxification of any obstructions to the fulfillment of one's life purpose. This is a cleansing of the entire hara line and can be a quite intense, deep emotional purging. Healers who have experienced this chakra have called it the "garbage chakra" or the "vomit chakra." The process is ultimately positive but may not seem so at the time. Go through it by simply allowing it to happen. Watch the sensations and let them go, neither fighting, resisting nor trying to change them. Welcome the clearing and send love.

The next primary center on the hara line is the *hara chakra*, or the hara itself. It has been known in Asia from ancient times, and is located about two and a half inches below the navel, above the kundalini belly chakra. Its color is *golden* to orange-brown in color but may deepen in healing, even turning hot and red. A number of orangy-gold flowers and gemstones activate the hara. In Asia, all energy work starts and ends at this center, which is the source of incarnation and the place from which the life force emanates to the rest of the body. The hara chakra connects one's will to live with the life sustaining energy of the Earth and the Earth chakra (see below). Strength, power, life force, and regenerative ability also originate from this center when the chakra is fully grounded to the Earth.

The deep ruby or *maroon perineum chakra* is next. This energy point is located (on the emotional body) between the openings of the vagina and the anus, where episiotomies are performed in childbirth. This is the energy gate through which the Earth Ch'i life force is brought into the body and held for distribution at the hara center. In Ch'i Kung, it is called "the gateway of life and death." The perineum is the place of activating and anchoring one's life intention and purpose into physical plane reality. A number of deep red flowers but only a few gemstones activate this chakra.

A pair of small chakras is located behind the knees. Called *movement chakras*, they direct one's movement forward on one's life path. People who have resistance or difficulty in fulfilling their life purpose may have pain in their knees, and the color-matching gemstones are usually *tan* or *forest green*. Below the knee chakras, in the soles of the feet, is another chakra pair. These are called *grounding chakras*, and their color is *brown*. This chakra pair centers one's life purpose into physical direction and manifestation. A very few unusually colored flowers and some gemstones serve these chakra pairs.

The energy line begun at the transpersonal point moves vertically through the body and enters deep into the Earth, as deep as the person can ground herself into the planet and root her intention for being here. The chakra that roots the hara line into Goddess Earth is called the *Earth chakra*, or Earth Star. I see its color as *shiny black*, and some deep red flowers with black gemstones are possible to activate it. The chakra anchors the incarnation/lifetime into earthplane reality, makes this planet one's home, and places one's life purpose into an Earthly context. This ending of the hara line is the grounding and ballast for one's lifetime and life purpose.

Besides the chakras, the hara line itself is comprised of a double flow of energy. One channel moves from the perineum chakra up the back, over the top of the head, and down the face to the upper lip. In acupuncture and Ch'i Kung, this channel is called the Governor Channel. The second energy flow starts at the lower lip and descends down the front of the body to end at the perineum. This is called the Conception Vessel. Auxiliary flows move energy through the legs and arms into these channels. Ch'i Kung is the ancient energy discipline that develops the hara channels and chakras, similar to yoga that works with the kundalini line. A few flowers and gems in varying colors activate the flows.

The emotions are central to today's healing issues and needs, and the hara line chakras offer access to achieving profound emotional healing. Flower and gemstone essences that match the hara line chakras provide direct entry into the emotional body and through it to the outer energy bodies for core soul healing. The ability to have that access is a major healing breakthrough.

Growing Your Own Flowers

Growing your own flowers with the aid of nature devas is another step in making and using flower essences. A trip to any garden center provides more plant choices suitable for your climate than any one garden can grow. Get to know the needs of the flowers you are attracted to before bringing them home. Plants requiring full sun do poorly in shaded yards, and shade-loving species may fail in full sunshine. Decide whether you wish to plant annuals that must be replaced yearly, biennials that bloom in their second year and then die, or perennials that are relatively permanent. Do you wish to start your garden with seeds, started seedlings, or more fully grown plants? Would you like, and can you maintain, a water garden? If you have the space for flowering trees, the Earth needs them, but inquire before buying as to just how big the tree will get.

Similar to the way I make essences, I like to bring new plants into my garden in the waxing phase of the moon, from the New Moon until just after the Full. Plant annuals at this time also and any plants that produce above-ground crops (such as flowers). On the waning moon, from a few days past the Full until a week before the New Moon, plant bulbs, biennials, nonflowering perennials, and any other plants that produce crops below the ground. A waxing moon feeds the leaves and blossoms, and a waning moon the bulbs and roots. The last quarter is generally considered barren and is not for planting but for cultivating, weeding, and eliminating pests. When the waxing moon is in Cancer, the planting of all crops is favored; a waxing moon in Libra is excellent for planting flowers and flowering vines, and vines also grow well when planted with the waxing moon in Scorpio.[11] Make sure that the last frost has passed and that the timing is favorable in your climate before planting.

Every yard and home has an overlighting deva who can be contacted to help the growth of your garden. The Goddesses Flora, Aphrodite, and Persephone also love flowers. Each plant has its deva as well. The life force energies of trees are called dryads. Dryads are wise and ancient, even those connected to young trees. Make an effort to contact these Be-ings, welcoming them into your life and garden, and asking their help in your flowers' cultivation and growth. Do this in the meditative state while sitting near the plants, and check in with them often. Ask their advice and help on every aspect of gardening and cooperate with them fully. If you treat these Be-ings with affection and respect, they will grant you the flowers of your dreams.

The Findhorn Garden in Scotland was begun in 1962 and was the first known modern garden developed in co-creation with the devas. A barren place of gravel and sand, with no topsoil and only gorse growing, Findhorn became a green showplace in a few short years. The ability of Dorothy Maclean and Eileen Caddy to speak with the devas of the land and plants, and Peter Caddy's willingness to do as they directed, brought spectacular results quickly. The Findhorn Garden used no pesticides or chemical fertilizers whatsoever, but was cultivated totally by organic methods. Respect for life—the life of the plants, soil, the plant devas, and those who ate the garden harvest was paramount. The garden produced huge vegetables and oversized flowers from around the world, even growing prize roses despite the poor soil.

Every garden can be a co-creative one like Findhorn's, and if the flowers are not nine feet high, they will at least be healthy and beautiful. The secrets lie in cooperation with the devas and using organic methods that enrich the soil, rather than chemicals that deplete the Earth. Instead of chemical fertilizers, use aged manure and peat moss when planting, and start a compost bin. Make a square board frame about three feet wide and three feet deep. Place it outdoors and put in it yard clippings, pulled weeds, kitchen salad peelings, herbal tea dregs, coffee grounds, and egg shells. Do not use pet manures, treated paper, or meat scraps. Cover each layer of greens and scraps with a layer of potting soil, wet the bin weekly, and stir it with a rake about every three weeks. In about three months the compost is ready; dig it into the soil around your plants. Cooled coffee grounds can be put around plant roots on top of the soil, and a layer of mulch around plant roots helps to protect them from pests.

Pests can be treated in ways respectful to the Earth, too. No garden is without at least some of them, so first decide if they are truly doing harm before working to remove them, and remember that some insects are allies. Pick caterpillars from plants by hand, dropping them into soapy water. Use pheromone traps and barriers, water and soapy water sprays, diatomaceous Earth, baking soda, and helpful insect predators like ladybugs, lacewings, nematodes, and parasitic wasps.

These can be bought at organic garden centers or ordered by mail. If further control is needed, use organic bacillus-based sprays that target the pest without polluting the plants or planet. The best known of these is Bt (*Bacillus thuringiensis*) for caterpillars, which is sold widely under a number of names. Try copper sulfate instead of chemical fungicides. Use chemicals only when absolutely necessary and when no organic alternative is possible.

Information on these methods can be gained at local garden centers (many of which are becoming organically aware), your state Agricultural Extension Service, and from a variety of books. Some places to start are the Sunset garden series, especially Sunset's *Garden Pests & Diseases* (Sunset Publishing Group, 1993) and *Organic Flower Gardening* Magazine (Rodale Press). An increasing number of other books and publications are becoming available as more and more people are protecting the Earth by developing this awareness.

It is important to make your flower essences from plants that are not contaminated by toxic chemicals and pesticides. (And of course, never use poisonous plants.) Though very little if any of the physical plant matter actually goes into the flower essence, chemical residues in the essences may be unsafe. Flower essences are natural healing methods that are best taken from naturally grown plants. When you use organic cultivation and pest elimination, the devas and dryads of your garden will also help you control the pests and grow strong plants. Plants healthy with good care and nutrition, like healthy people and pets, are largely resistant to pests and dis-ease.

This book is a beginner's guide to making and using flower and gemstone essences. It is only the beginning of a holistic healing field. Essences offer emotional support and emotional/mental/spiritual healing. They stabilize, cleanse, and soothe, promote spiritual growth and core soul healing, and foster positive change and inner peace. Use them well with the blessings of the Goddess, and make and use them with beauty and joy. A selection of flower and gemstone essence combinations follows.

Two Hundred and One Flower and Gemstone Essence Combinations

Abundance Essence

Flower: Goldenrain Tree (Koelreuteria formosana), yellow
Gemstones: Pyrite, Emerald, Peridot, Danburite, Clear Quartz Crystal
Chakra: Solar plexus

- Promotes prosperity, abundance, success, deserving
- Enhances ability to receive and to manifest
- Brings balanced inner power, good luck, good planning ability
- Heals ulcers

Acceptance Essence

Flower: Hollyhock (Alcea Rosa), white
Gemstones: Turquoise, Aquamarine, Gem Silica, Danburite, Clear Quartz Crystal
Chakra: Thymus

- Heals grief and sorrow from the past
- Eases living in the past, holding onto old pain and past hurts
- Releases despair, depression, and hopelessness
- Replaces anger with acceptance, aids loneliness
- Completes the mourning process, promotes going forward and going on

Aging Essence

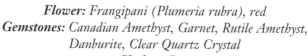

Flower: *Bougainvillea (Bougainvillea spp.), white*
Gemstones: *Pearl, White Opal, Clear Fluorite, Danburite,
Herkimer Diamond*
Chakra: *Transpersonal point*

- Supports transformations: acceptance of aging, change, and death
- Strengthens emotional support for all stress
- Promotes connection with guides, angels, and Goddess
- Encourages trust in the process of life and age, wisdom and growth, inner peace
- Inspires joyful old age

Amazon Essence I

Flower: *Frangipani (Plumeria rubra), red*
Gemstones: *Canadian Amethyst, Garnet, Rutile Amethyst,
Danburite, Clear Quartz Crystal*
Chakra: *Root*

- Increases female active energy, balances action with receptivity
- Encourages assertiveness without aggression, heals shyness and fear of expressing one's needs
- Balances yin and yang in women, aids expressing anger safely, offers courage

Amazon Essence II

— ❀ —

Flower: *Frangipani (Plumeria rubra), white*
Gemstones: *Moonstone, Pearl, Garnet, Danburite, Clear Quartz Crystal*
Chakra: *Crown*

- Increases female receptive energy
- Balances over-action, calms aggressiveness, aids in asserting one's needs calmly, promotes ability to express anger safely
- Fosters stability and gentleness, increases yin in women

Ancient Wisdom Essence

— ❀ —

Flower: *Water Lily (Nymphae spp.), purple*
Gemstones: *Amethyst, Purple Fluorite, Selenite, Danburite, Herkimer Diamond*
Chakra: *Crown*

- Transcends suffering to attain spiritual wisdom, aids in becoming an old soul
- Evokes guidance from oversoul, angels, and spirit guides; increases spiritual growth
- Supports transformations, aids in attaining enlightenment in this lifetime and in fulfilling karmic obligations

Angel Essence

———— ❖ ————

Flower: Sky Vine (Thunbergia grandiflora), white
Gemstones: Phenacite, Moonstone, Angelite, Danburite, Herkimer Diamond
Chakra: Transpersonal point

- Increases energy, healing, and unconditional love from angelic realms
- Promotes connection with angels, aids in channeling angel energy and creativity, increases knowledge of oversoul/angel within
- Enables all-healing and soul level healing; transforms negative karma, repairs twelve-strand DNA

Angelic Grace Essence

———— ❖ ————

Flower: Rose—Angel Face (Rosa spp.), lavender pink
Gemstones: Kunzite, Rose Quartz, Selenite, Danburite, Herkimer Diamond
Chakra: Heart

- Increases awareness of angelic presence and the angelic realm, facilitates contact with one's personal angels, inspires divine guidance
- Brings grace, forgiveness, compassion, universal love, self-love, heart healing, inner peace

Anger Essence

———— ❀ ————

Flower: *Bromeliad (Bromeliaceae), red*
Gemstones: *Ruby, Rubellite (Dark Pink Tourmaline), Black Tourmaline,*
Danburite, Clear Quartz Crystal
Chakra: *Root*

- Transforms and heals anger; releases rage, resentment, depression
- Asserts life force and the will to live
- Fosters compassion
- Heals blood dis-eases, lung dis-eases, anemia, AIDS

Aphrodite Essence

———— ❀ ————

Flower: *Camellia (Camellia japonica), red*
Gemstones: *Garnet, Red Coral, Jet, Danburite, Herkimer Diamond*
Chakra: *Root*

- Heals lost love and draws new love in; heals grief, heart–ache, heartbreak, broken relationships
- Strengthens the ability to open to new love, stabilizes new relationships and unions
- Aids success in marriage, brings about compatible sexuality and lovers' bonding

Archangel Essence

Flower: Wisteria *(Wisteria sinensis), blue*
Gemstones: Lapis Lazuli, Blue Aventurine, Angelite,
Danburite, Clear Quartz Crystal
Chakra: Third *eye*

- Aids ability to contact and communicate with highest level angelic presences, spirit guides, other-planetary healers and helpers, one's oversoul, and the Goddess
- Aids psychic opening, psychic healing, and self-healing; develops clairvoyance, clairaudience, and channeling
- Aids in becoming a channel for highest level psychic healing and information; promotes entrance to the light body, mind grid, Earth grid, and intergalactic grid

Ariel's Essence

Flower: Sky Vine *(Thunbergia grandiflora), white*
Gemstones: Chrysoprase, Green Jade, Emerald, Danburite,
Herkimer Diamond
Chakra: Heart

- Accesses angels, angelic wisdom, the angelic realm; helps in finding your wings and in finding the angel within/oversoul
- Encourages all-healing, soul body healing; repairs damage at all aura body levels
- Brings inner peace, love for all life

Ascension Essence

— ❀ —

Flower: Hyacinth (Hyacinthus orientalis), white
Gemstones: Moonstone, White Opal, Selenite, Danburite, Herkimer Diamond
Chakra: Transpersonal point

- Channels other-dimensional aid into the four bodies (physical, emotional, mental, spiritual)
- Promotes contact with healing and healers from other dimensions, realms, and planets
- Opens and clears kundalini and hara line chakras and energy flows
- Repairs core soul damage, soul fragmentation, twelve-strand DNA; aids ascension

Assimilation Essence

— ❀ —

Flower: Cuban Buttercup, yellow
Gemstones: Golden Topaz, Yellow Apatite, Natural Citrine,
Danburite, Clear Quartz Crystal
Chakra: Diaphragm

- Cleanses, clears, and releases; catalyzes inner change, inner growth, and life transitions
- Activates and escalates vibrational energy, supports energy shifts, aligns the energy bodies
- Clears and opens the light body, aids assimilation in all forms
- Helps nausea and digestive upsets, is calming

Astarte Essence

———— ❁ ————

Flower: *Rose—Perfume Beauty (Rosa spp.), pink*
Gemstones: *Pink Tourmaline, Pink Kunzite, Amethyst,*
Danburite, Clear Quartz Crystal
Chakra: Heart

- Helps in attracting and sustaining love and union, promotes union of body and soul
- Enhances soul mate relationships, deepens mutual love and openness between lovers
- Increases empathy, caring, unconditional love, fidelity
- Strengthens true marriage, brings about harmonious and peaceful relationships, lifelong relationships

Astral Essence

———— ❁ ————

Flower: *Yarrow (Achillea), pink*
Gemstones: *Kunzite, Pink Tourmaline, Morganite,*
Danburite, Clear Quartz Crystal
Chakra: Heart

- Heals and protects the vulnerable heart, inspires this-life and past-life emotional healing
- Releases heart scars
- Encourages emotional and astral body healing, brings the astral double into the physical body
- Engenders safety and security, joy

Aura Essence

Flower: Hibiscus *(Hibiscus rosa sinensis), yellow*
Gemstones: Sunstone, Natural Citrine, Golden Beryl
or Topaz, Danburite, Clear Quartz Crystal
Chakra: Diaphragm

- Cleanses the aura and subtle bodies, releases entities and attachments, heals tears in aura and subtle bodies
- Clears and expands energy field
- Asserts positivity and inner peace
- Aids arthritis

Aura Cleansing Essence

Flower: Allamanda *(Allamanda spp.), purple*
Gemstones: Rutile Amethyst, Selenite, Moonstone,
Danburite, Clear Quartz Crystal
Chakra: Transpersonal point

- Expands spiritual truth, cleanses and heals the spiritual body
- Opens and validates spirituality, facilitates all-aura cleansing and healing
- Helps to access highest level guidance, stimulates psychic amplification
- Brings certainty of Goddess

Awareness Essence

— ❖ —

Flower: Hyacinth *(Hyacinthus orientalis), blue*
Gemstones: Holly Blue Agate, Blue Lace Agate, Kyanite,
Danburite, Herkimer Diamond
Chakra: *Causal body*

- Opens and reinforces conscious awareness of other dimensions, heals soul fragmentation and core soul damage
- Eases the entrance into the mind, Earth, and galactic grids; increases planetary and interplanetary awareness
- Aids channeling/receiving spirit guides, angels, and other-planetary helpers and healers; aids channelers, healers, and Earth healers

Beloved Essence

— ❖ —

Flower: Confederate Jasmine *(Trachelospermum jasminoides), white*
Gemstones: Peach Aventurine, Peach or White Moonstone, Orange
Sunstone or Carnelian, Danburite, Herkimer Diamond
Chakra: *Hara*

- Brings about fulfillment of union of body and soul, leads to love's consummation in the physical
- Connects twin souls, brings harmony and total peace together, supports marriage for life and beyond
- Enhances karmic healing between lovers and life mates, strengthens mutual commitment

Birth Essence

———— ❀ ————

Flower: *Bougainvillea (Bougainvillea sp.), light pink*
Gemstones: *Gem Rose Quartz, Pink Kunzite, Cobaltite,*
Danburite, Clear Quartz Crystal
Chakra: *Heart*

- Assists birth and giving birth, eases welcoming to the world, soothes infants and new mothers
- Helps bring soul into body
- Fosters physical, emotional, and spiritual growth
- Stimulates milk production

Blessing Essence

———— ❀ ————

Flower: *Cosmos (Cosmos spp.), multicolored combination*
Gemstones: *Turquoise, Aquamarine, Emerald, Danburite,*
Clear Quartz Crystal
Chakra: *Thymus*

- Honors the oneness of all life, teaches self-blessing and blessing of others
- Furthers giving and receiving, promotes harmony in groups
- Fosters animal communication
- Increases forgiveness, heals guilt and blame, heals grief, creates joy

Blood Building Essence

— ❁ —

Flower: Christmas Plant/ Florida Poincetta (Euphurbia spp.), red/green
Gemstones: Bloodstone, Pyrite, Hematite, Danburite, Clear Quartz Crystal
Chakra: Root

- Builds and strengthens the blood
- Heals hemorrhaging, anemia, wounds; reduces excessive menstrual bleeding
- Gives courage, inner strength, determination
- Grounds kundalini reactions, grounds psychic opening

Blood Cleansing Essence

— ❁ —

Flower: Ixora (Ixora coccinea), red
Gemstones: Bloodstone, Azurite, Black Tourmaline,
Emerald, Danburite, Clear Quartz Crystal
Chakra: Root

- Cleanses the blood; aids in healing infectious dis-eases, HIV/AIDS, intestinal dis-eases, cancer, leukemia
- Establishes clear sexual boundaries, promotes sexual healing

Bodhisattva Essence

— ❋ —

Flower: Bleeding Heart (Clerodendrum thomsoniae), white/red
Gemstones: Garnet, Moonstone, Pink Tourmaline (Rubellite),
Danburite, Clear Quartz Crystal
Chakra: Causal body

- Supports the bodhisattvas, healers, and planetary servers; helps those who give too much of themselves for others' sake
- Aids in overcoming burnout, depletion, exhaustion, depression, and despair
- Offers hope, strength, and grounding in the now; promotes regeneration

Body and Soul Essence

— ❋ —

Flower: PowderPuff (Calliandra haematocephala), red
Gemstones: Rose Quartz, Pink Tourmaline, Garnet,
Danburite, Clear Quartz Crystal
Chakra: Perineum

- Increases security in one's appearance, enhances self-image
- Teaches that "You are Goddess"
- Reinforces being in body and respecting the body
- Eases incarnation, develops awareness of the soul

Brede's Essence

———— ❊ ————

Flower: *Sky Vine (Thunbergia grandiflora), blue*
Gemstones: *Sapphire, Angelite, Blue Aventurine, Azurite,*
Danburite, Clear Quartz Crystal
Chakra: *Throat*

- Brings about all healing, Earth healing, gentle transformation; eases life changes
- Furthers peace of mind, happiness, creativity; aids in expressing one's truths
- Promotes spiritual growth, aids reception to guides and channeling
- Furthers psychic healing and contact with the Goddess and Goddess within

Cassandra Essence:

———— ❊ ————

Flower: *Crossandra Plant (Crossandra infundibuliformis), orange*
Gemstones: *Orange Sunstone, Yellow Sunstone, Peach or White*
Moonstone, Danburite, Herkimer Diamond
Chakra: *Hara*

- Opens and expands clairvoyance, advances psychic ability and channeling
- Enhances communication with guides and angels, increases light and Goddess energy
- Supports new psychics and beginning channelers, promotes self-confidence in one's abilities and in the psychic realm, protects psychics from negative interference

Chakra Essence

──── ❀ ────

Flower: Hibiscus (Hibiscus rosa sinensis), one each of red, peach, yellow, rose, white
Gemstones: Garnet, Carnelian, Natural Citrine, Rose Quartz, Amethyst, Danburite, Clear Quartz Crystal
Chakra: All aura

- Opens and balances the kundalini chakras; stabilizes the physical body, etheric double, and emotional body
- Encourages spiritual development, fosters all healing, calms, balances energy

Changing Woman Essence

──── ❀ ────

Flower: Mandevilla (Mandevilla splendens), pink
Gemstones: Crystalline Rose Quartz, Pink Kunzite, Pink Tourmaline, Danburite, Clear Quartz Crystal
Chakra: Heart

- Heals the heart, promotes emotional healing and release
- Releases heart scars, heals past and current abuse, heals past-life abuse
- Aids in changing karmic patterns
- Brings positive self-worth, joy in living

Channeling Essence I

— ❀ —

Flower: Angel's Trumpet Datura (Datura spp.), white
Gemstones: Moonstone, Angelite, Azurite, Danburite,
Clear Quartz Crystal (phenacite-optional)
Chakra: Transpersonal point

- Expands connection with guides, Goddess, angels
- Furthers channeling, mediumship, meditation, astral travel, star wisdom
- Accesses soul level healing, spiritual awareness, repairs DNA

Channeling Essence II

— ❀ —

Flower: King's Mantle (Thunbergia erecta), purple/gold
Gemstones: Rutile Amethyst, Ametrine, Rutile Citrine (natural),
Danburite, Clear Quartz Crystal (phenacite-optional)
Chakra: Crown

- Balances spiritual opening with daily living, and the psychic realm with the conscious mind
- Calms new psychics and those experiencing an acceleration of psychic energies
- Aids those who fear their psychic knowledge, stabilizes new channelers

Ch'i Kung Essence

———— ❀ ————

Flower: Ixora (Ixora coccinea), yellow
Gemstones: Natural Citrine, Golden Topaz, Amber, Danburite,
Clear Quartz Crystal
Chakra: Solar plexus

- Balances meridian system, opens meridian blocks, and frees energy flows
- Opens and heals hara line and light body
- Brings mental cleansing, balances the mental body, aids intellect
- Balances energy, heals exhaustion and depression

Children's Essence

———— ❀ ————

Flower: Portulaca (Portulaca grandiflora), pink
Gemstones: Rose Quartz, Pink Smithsonite, Kunzite,
Danburite, Clear Quartz Crystal
Chakra: Heart

- Aids and supports children in learning about the world, helps make going to school positive, aids in making friends
- Encourages learning from plants, animals, stones, and people
- Aids in dealing with hurts and traumas on all levels
- Protects innocence, cushions and eases the fear and sorrows of childhood

Circus Essence

--- ❈ ---

Flower: *Portulaca (Portulaca grandiflora), mixed colors*
Gemstones: *Orange Calcite, Rose Quartz, Golden Topaz,*
Danburite, Clear Quartz Crystal
Chakras: *Belly, Solar plexus, and Heart*

- Brings laughter and joy back to one's life
- Heals traumas and transitions, reduces disappointment and heartache
- Expands opening to the Goddess' gifts, fosters appreciation of the beauty of one's life and the Earth
- Turns grief, depression, guilt, or self-blame into acceptance, validation, and inner peace

Clairvoyance Essence

--- ❈ ---

Flower: *Blue Violet (Viola odorata), indigo*
Gemstones: *Lapis Lazuli, Blue Aventurine, Azurite,*
Danburite, Clear Quartz Crystal
Chakra: *Third eye*

- Increases spiritual truth and sense of purpose, facilitates psychic and spiritual opening
- Magnifies integrity, clairvoyance, and clairaudience; encourages mediumship
- Aids contact with spirit guides; brings connection with Goddess, mental body, and grid
- Attunes the light body, promotes lymphatic cleansing, balances the meridians

Clarity Essence

— ❁ —

Flower: Portulaca (Portulaca grandiflora), yellow
Gemstones: Amber Calcite, Golden Topaz, Rutile Citrine,
Danburite, Clear Quartz Crystal
Chakra: Solar plexus

- Calms and stabilizes the mind, brings mental clarity, heals the mental body
- Acts as an intellectual stimulant, aids ability to make clear choices and decisions, furthers assimilation of ideas and information
- Heals depression, mental dis-eases, confusion, memory loss

Cleansing Essence

— ❁ —

Flower: Dandelion (Tarafacum), yellow
Gemstones: Natural Citrine, Peridot, Amber Calcite,
Danburite, Clear Quartz Crystal
Chakra: Diaphragm

- Cleanses emotional body, releases old emotions from this and past lives
- Fosters healing the past and moving forward
- Balances energy, aids body pain, relaxes muscle tension, soothes digestion, heals urinary dis-eases

Comfort Essence

———— ❈ ————

Flower: Lisianthus (Lisianthus spp.), purple
Gemstones: Rutile Amethyst, Sugilite, Lepidolite, Moonstone,
Danburite, Clear Quartz Crystal
Chakra: *Crown*

- Calms, aids insomnia, quiets the mind
- Teaches trust in Goddess, heals past and past-life traumas
- Brings peace, spiritual healing
- Helps headaches and migraines, reduces fear

Conscious Dying Essence

———— ❈ ————

Flower: Golden Chalice (Solandra nitida zucs.) or
Angel Trumpet Datura (Datura metel), yellow
Gemstones: Golden Topaz, Amber Calcite, Golden Beryl or Yellow Fluorite,
Danburite, Herkimer Diamond
Chakra: *Solar plexus*

- Supports conscious dying, peaceful transition; brings awareness of guides and angels in death passage
- Helps attain enlightenment at time of death, releases the body
- Rebalances after a near death experience

Courage Essence

———— ❁ ————

Flower: Century Plant *(Agave americana), orange*
Gemstones: *Pecos Quartz, Carnelian, Orange Agate,*
Danburite, Clear Quartz Crystal
Chakra: *Hara*

- Brings courage to follow one's life path despite any difficulty, develops strength, increases awareness of life purpose and self-awareness
- Ends victimization and trauma of abuse situations, heals past abuse, releases anger

Creation Essence

———— ❁ ————

Flower: Lily—Spider *(Hymenocallis spp.), white*
Gemstones: *Amethyst, Gem Silica, Larimar,*
Danburite, Clear Quartz Crystal
Chakra: *Throat*

- Enhances creativity, artistry; opens artist's block
- Aids channeling; provides inspiration; aids connection with guides, muses, and Goddess
- Calms, heals headaches and migraines, reduces stress

Crown Essence

———— ❖ ————

Flower: Rose—Reine des Violettes (Rosa spp.), purple
Gemstones: Rutile Amethyst, Pink or Violet Tourmaline, Blue Labradorite, Danburite, Herkimer Diamond
Chakra: Crown

- Opens and clears kundalini and hara line channels and chakras, clears energy blockages
- Removes negative interference including alien implants, releases possessions and negative entities, releases psychic attacks
- Accesses positive intergalactic healers and helpers for protection from interference and attack

Crown Jewels Essence

———— ❖ ————

Flower: Shrimp Plant (Beloperone guttata), white
Gemstones: Pearl, Moonstone, White Opal, Danburite, Clear Quartz Crystal
Chakra: Transpersonal point

- Balances all chakras and full aura
- Eases kundalini opening and psychic opening, eases rapid psychic development
- Soothes transition states, heals body of light, promotes core soul healing and clearing
- Clears negativity, repairs twelve-strand DNA

Cupid Essence

Flower: Orange Blossom *(Citrus sinensis), white*
Gemstones: Pink Kunzite, Rose Quartz, Cobaltite, Danburite,
Clear Quartz Crystal
Chakra: *Heart*

- Calms, brings clarity, engenders trust
- Supports emotional release, heals heart scars, aids heart healing
- Helps one to "follow your heart"
- Sustains enlightened relationships, releases codependency, fosters self-love
- Eases depression and anxiety

Detox Essence

Flower: Allamanda/ Golden Bells *(Allamanda cathartica), yellow*
Gemstones: Natural Citrine, Amber Calcite, Golden Topaz,
Danburite, Clear Quartz Crystal
Chakra: *Solar plexus*

- Cleanses, detoxifies, supports one to stop smoking
- Heals food, drug, alcohol, and prescription drug addictions
- Reduces obsessions, changes negative habits
- Brings about emotional clarity, inner truth

Deva Essence

———— ❃ ————

Flower: Honeysuckle (Lonicera sempervirens), pink
Gemstones: Pink Kunzite, Cobaltite, Pink Tourmaline,
Danburite, Clear Quartz Crystal
Chakra: Heart

- Aids contact and communication with fairies and devas
- Brings childlike sweetness and joy into one's life
- Increases innocence, gentleness; aids in being gentle and loving with others
- Brings about openness, creates emotional protection and security
- Calms, protects dreams and dreamwork

Devotion Essence

———— ❃ ————

Flower: Crape Myrtle (Lagerstroemia indica), lavender
Gemstones: Amethyst, Sugilite, Pink Tourmaline,
Danburite, Clear Quartz Crystal
Chakra: Crown

- Brings about union of intellect and emotion
- Calms; steadies; fosters responsibility, sobriety, self-acceptance
- Increases unconditional love and self-love, deepens devotion, aids meditation

Earth Essence

———— ❁ ————

Flower: Water Lily (Nymphae spp.), white
Gemstones: Andean Opal, Gem Silica, Blue Aventurine,
Danburite, Herkimer Diamond
Chakra: Throat

- Brings Earth awareness, aids Earth healers, increases awareness of planetary stewardship
- Honors the oneness of all life, engenders compassion for all that lives
- Facilitates telepathy with devas, elementals, dolphins, water spirits, and Earth spirits
- Encourages participation in Earth changes; supports healing for oneself, others, and the planet
- Supports incarnated bodhisattvas, aids psychic ability, heals psychics' burnout

Earth Changes Essence

———— ❁ ————

Flower: Hyacinth (Hyacinthus spp.), red
Gemstones: Star Ruby, Garnet, Kyanite, Danburite, Herkimer Diamond
Chakra: Causal body

- Opens one's conscious awareness as a channel for Earth healing via other dimensions
- Heals soul level damage in oneself and others (via psychic healing)
- Heals soul fragmentation, repairs DNA, helps maintain one's stability during Earth changes energy shifts
- Opens intergalactic contact with Earth change healers and helpers for oneself, other people, and the planet

Earth Love Essence

— ❈ —

Flower: *Gloxinia (Sinnimgia speciosa), fuchsia*
Gemstones: *Cobaltite, Pink Tourmaline, Rose Quartz,*
Danburite, Clear Quartz Crystal
Chakra: *Heart*

- Brings love and universal love onto the earthplane, aids the Earth changes by channeling love and healing
- Promotes being a transmitter of love for planetary growth and change, promotes peace by holding and keeping peace in oneself, aids self-love and love for others

Earth Walk Essence I

— ❈ —

Flower: *Gloxinia (Sinnimgia speciosa), maroon/white*
Gemstones: *Garnet, Rutile Amethyst, Black Kyanite,*
Danburite, Clear Quartz Crystal
Chakra: *Perineum*

- Connects the hara and kundalini energy flows, Earth and sky, root and crown
- Aids balance of earthplane groundedness with spiritual purpose and awareness
- Leads to walking on Mother Earth as an aware spiritual Be-ing
- Helps Earth healers to remain in balance while channeling psychic energy, grounds and centers

Earth Walk Essence II

———— ❀ ————

Flower: Gloxinia (Sinnimgia speciosa), purple/white
Gemstones: Rutile Amethyst, Moonstone, Labradorite,
Danburite, Clear Quartz Crystal
Chakra: *Crown*

- Stimulates psychic vision and out-of-body travel
- Aids seeing psychically for healing and Earth healing, aids distance/psychic healing
- Helps in understanding and stabilization during the Earth changes, aids Earth healers and those helping souls to pass over
- Aids in holding and channeling psychic energy

Easy Essence

———— ❀ ————

Flower: Jacobinia (Jacobinia spp.), pink
Gemstones: Pink Tourmaline, Pink Kunzite, Moonstone,
Danburite, Herkimer Diamond
Chakra: *Heart*

- Promotes heart's ease, peace of mind and heart, brings heart healing, heart blooming
- Increases joy and the ability to express love, sensitizes the ability to feel emotions in self and others

Emotional Healing Essence

Flower: *Trumpet Creeper (Campsis radicans), orange*
Gemstones: *Pecos Quartz, Phantom Quartz, Moonstone,*
Danburite, Clear Quartz Crystal
Chakra: *Belly*

- Releases anger, emotional traumas, sexual and emotional abuse
- Heals sexual dysfunction, clears old emotions
- Helps asthma, arthritis, bursitis

Energy Essence

Flower: *Trumpet Creeper (Campis radicans), yellow*
Gemstones: *Yellow Sunstone, Golden Topaz, Natural Citrine,*
Danburite, Clear Quartz Crystal
Chakra: *Solar plexus*

- Aids inner cleansing, clears crystals, releases spirit attachments and entities
- Offers protection, stabilizes energy flows, aids astral travel, balances psychic opening
- Aids digestion; strengthens gall bladder, urinary tract

Energy Purification Essence I

———— ❀ ————

Flower: *Clematis (Clematis spp.), dark blue*
Gemstones: *Azurite, Blue Aventurine, Celestite,*
Danburite, Herkimer Diamond
Chakra: *Third eye*

- Furthers energy cleansing and purification of hara and kundalini channels and chakras
- Clears obstructions, aids inability to move forward, alleviates being stuck
- Promotes mental transformation and change, stimulates mental body and light body healing
- Removes emotional attachments and negative thought forms, heals negative karmic patterns
- Aids psychic development and insight

Energy Purification Essence II

———— ❀ ————

Flower: *Clematis (Clematis spp.), dark red*
Gemstones: *Garnet, Black Kyanite, Obsidian, Danburite,*
Clear Quartz Crystal
Chakra: *Earth*

- Helps with energy cleansing and purification of hara and kundalini channels and chakras
- Clears obstructions, aids inability to move forward on one's earthly path
- Connects one's spiritual life purpose with earthplane action and competence
- Removes indecisiveness and uncertainty, aids earthplane oriented change and transformation

- Heals fear, clears and heals the etheric body for physical body healing

Enlightenment Essence

———— ❧ ————

Flower: Water Lily (Nymphae spp.), white
Gemstones: Selenite, Moonstone, Clear Beryl (Goshenite),
Danburite, Clear Quartz Crystal
Chakra: Transpersonal point

- Clears all bodies and aura levels, opens and aligns the astral body and body of light
- Clears chakra blocks, releases negative attachments and entities, releases past-life artifacts
- Heals negativity, fills aura and bodies with light/information/healing, increases one's connection with Goddess
- Aids karmic clearing and release, repairs twelve-strand DNA, regenerates at all levels

Eternity Essence

———— ❧ ————

Flower: Crape Myrtle (Lagerstroemia indica), white
Gemstones: Moonstone, Diamond, Rutile Quartz,
Danburite, Clear Quartz Crystal
Chakra: Transpersonal point

- Strengthens marriage for life and beyond; strengthens union, fidelity, truth, and trust in relationship; deepens soul bonding
- Manifests love that is total and eternal, encourages unconditional love, draws soul mates

Fairy Essence

———— ❀ ————

Flower: *Chinese Lantern/ Clammy Ground Cherry*
(Physalis heterophylla), yellow
Gemstones: *Moonstone, Emerald or Green Tourmaline, Blue Sapphire,*
Danburite, Clear Quartz Crystal
Chakra: *Solar plexus*

- Increases perception of fairies and nature devas, brings Earth awareness, aids telepathy with animals and plants
- Clears crystals and gemstones, clears land of past traumas and entities

Family of Womon Essence

———— ❀ ————

Flower: *Rainbow Cassia (Cassia fistula), peach/gold*
Gemstones: *Natural Citrine, Peach or Rainbow Moonstone, Rhodochrosite,*
Danburite, Clear Quartz Crystal
Chakra: *Heart*

- Reinforces opening to the Family of Woman; heals the damage of misogyny, racism, ablism, fat oppression, and homophobia in oneself and on the planet
- Heals the Earth of war, manifests a healed planet through one's heart

First Love Essence

Flower: *Portulaca (Portulaca grandiflora), fuchsia*
Gemstones: *Pink Tourmaline, Rose Quartz, Rhodonite,*
Danburite, Clear Quartz Crystal
Chakra: *Heart*

- Cushions and heals the process of falling in love for the first time or repeatedly
- Reinforces self-love, deepens the sense of reality about the other, helps to recognize real from wishful relationships
- Heals unrequited love, eases disappointment in first love, soothes puppy love
- Promotes sexual responsibility

Flight Essence

Flower: *Butterfly Weed (Asclepias tuberosa), orange*
Gemstones: *Carnelian, Amber, Orange Calcite, Danburite,*
Herkimer Diamond
Chakra: *Hara*

- Helps in finding one's wings and the ability to fly; furthers freedom; aids psychic flight, astral travel, meditation, shamanic journeys, star journeys
- Aids soul retrieval, facilitates core soul healing, repairs twelve-strand DNA
- Brings awareness of galactic origins, helps contact the living library within and the planetary grid without
- Stimulates awareness beyond Earth consciousness

Forever Essence

Flower: Yesterday, Today and Tomorrow (Brunfelcia), blue/pink/white
Gemstones: Angelite, Azurite, Blue Aventurine,
Danburite, Clear Quartz Crystal
Chakra: Third eye

- Breaks the bonds of the negative past, heals emotional and mental attachments and negative karmic patterns
- Heals from the etheric and celestial template level, aids access to angels and the Lords of Karma, fosters karmic release, core soul healing
- Revises the Akashic records, leads to breakthroughs and transformations

Forgiveness Essence

Flower: Bromeliad (Bromeliaceae), pink
Gemstones: Pink Kunzite, Rhodochrosite, Gem Rose Quartz,
Danburite, Clear Quartz Crystal
Chakra: Heart

- Unfolds heart secrets, heals past pain, brings emotional release
- Heals grief, shame, blame
- Allows speaking one's heart truths, helps in letting go, inspires forgiveness

Galaxy Essence

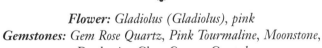

Flower: Water Lily *(Nymphae spp.), indigo*
Gemstones: Lapis Lazuli, Blue Aventurine, Azurite,
Danburite, Herkimer Diamond
Chakra: Third eye

- Helps one to receive the wisdom of the ancients, star wisdom, and wisdom from other galaxies and planets
- Expands channeling, psychic knowing, telepathy, and empathy
- Opens, clears, and heals the light body
- Brings about connection with the Earth grid and angelic realm, supports all healing

Gladness Essence

Flower: Gladiolus *(Gladiolus), pink*
Gemstones: Gem Rose Quartz, Pink Tourmaline, Moonstone,
Danburite, Clear Quartz Crystal
Chakra: Heart

- Brings gladness and joy into one's life, increases love of life
- Brings returned innocence, allows appreciation of simple pleasures
- Returns joy after painful times, hastens recovery from illness
- Increases will to continue one's life and life path, bolsters ability to love and love again

Goddess Within Essence

---- ❊ ----

Flower: *Azalea (Rhododendron spp.), white*
Gemstones: *Purple Fluorite, Aquamarine, Elestial Quartz,*
Herkimer Diamond, Clear Quartz Crystal
Chakra: *Crown*

- Manifests ascension—union of body and soul bodies, brings Goddess realization/Goddess within
- Increases inner knowing and peace, enhances spirituality, leads to inner growth and healing
- Connects with light body and oversoul, supports contact with spirit guides and mediumship

Golden Jewels Essence

---- ❊ ----

Flower: *Shrimp Plant (Beloperone guttata), yellow*
Gemstones: *Yellow Jade, Moonstone, Natural Citrine,*
Danburite, Clear Quartz Crystal
Chakra: *Solar plexus*

- Inspires positive pride, encourages acceptance of self, increases self-validation, promotes positive body image, self-confidence
- Helps in finding one's angels and wings
- Contributes to mastectomy/amputation recovery, calming

Golden Light Essence

———— ❈ ————

Flower: *Candle Bush (Cassia alata), yellow*
Gemstones: *Opal, Amber, Topaz, Danburite, Clear Quartz Crystal*
Chakra: *Solar plexus*

- Gives light in the darkness, invokes Goddess
- Balances chakras, aids in chakra clearing and opening
- Rejects negativity, clears entities and attachments

Good Old Days Essence

———— ❈ ————

Flower: *Rose—Wild Climbing Tea (Rosa spp.), pink*
Gemstones: *Gem Rose Quartz, Watermelon Tourmaline, Moonstone,*
Danburite, Clear Quartz Crystal
Chakra: *Heart*

- Heals the past, aids in remembering past lives and bringing the good old days to now
- Heals heart scars, heals the emotional body, promotes heart healing
- Changes sorrow into quiet joy; increases trust, acceptance

Green Jewels Essence

Flower: Shrimp Plant (Beloperone guttata), white
Gemstones: Green Tourmaline, Emerald, Moldavite,
Danburite, Clear Quartz Crystal
Chakra: Movement chakras

- Creates joyful movement on one's life path, brings knowledge of life purpose and ability to achieve it
- Increases joy and pride in one's purpose and movement
- Provides guidance on one's way, offers protection from delay and negativity, Green Tara's essence

Grief Essence

Flower: Peony (Paeonia lactiflora), white
Gemstones: Moonstone, Blue Topaz, Celestite,
Danburite, Clear Quartz Crystal
Chakra: Thymus

- Releases and heals grief and anger, helps one move through the stages of grieving
- Heals guilt, blame, and self-blame; promotes letting go; eases depression
- Increases awareness of immortality of the soul, brings inner peace, acceptance

Grounding Essence

Flower: *Bottle Brush Tree (Callisteman lanceolatus), red*
Gemstones: *Smoky Quartz, Garnet, Rutile Amethyst,*
Danburite, Clear Quartz Crystal
Chakra: *Root*

- Promotes grounding, living on the earthplane, increases security, strengthens roots, fosters responsibility
- Aids in letting go, brings physical independence
- Helps in intestinal cleansing, improving intestinal function, heals intestinal dis-eases and parasites

Happiness Essence

Flower: *Pink Poui Tree (Tabebuia pentaphylla), pink*
Gemstones: *Gem Rose Quartz, Morganite or Lepidolite,*
Pink Tourmaline, Danburite, Clear Quartz Crystal
Chakra: *Heart*

- Releases and heals karmic pain patterns; heals heart scars, emotional loss; eases despair, loneliness, grief
- Allows emotional and astral body healing
- Returns happiness to living, produces inner joy

Hara Essence

———— ❀ ————

Flower: *Silk Oak Tree (Grevillea robusta), orange*
Gemstones: *Amber, Red Jasper, Rhodochrosite, Danburite,*
Clear Quartz Crystal
Chakra: *Hara*

- Opens the hara and hara line, cleanses the hara line, strengthens life purpose
- Brings about sexual opening, helps achieve orgasm
- Increases the feeling of wanting to be here

Harmony Essence

———— ❀ ————

Flower: *Narcissus (Narcissus spp.), yellow/white*
Gemstones: *Yellow Fluorite, Rutile Citrine (natural), Moonstone,*
Danburite, Clear Quartz Crystal
Chakra: *Solar plexus*

- Increases self-confidence and brings a clear self-image, balanced ego
- Boosts clarity; supports positive boundaries; increases openness to others, caring and courtesy toward others and oneself
- Encourages consideration, cooperation, harmony with oneself and one's world

Hathor's Essence

Flower: Geranium (Geranium spp.), white
Gemstones: Moonstone, Selenite, White Opal, Danburite,
Clear Quartz Crystal
Chakra: Transpersonal point

- Increases opening to the Goddess and the Goddess within, strengthens women's connection to the moon and moon cycles
- Awakens spirituality and psychic ability, ritual enhancement; aids in Drawing Down the Moon
- Manifests strong expansion energy, calms and stabilizes psychic and spiritual growth
- Regulates menstrual cycles, promotes and regulates ovulation, eases menopause symptoms

Healer's Essence

Flower: Tree of Gold (Tabebuia argentea), yellow
Gemstones: Golden Topaz, Sunstone, Moonstone,
Danburite, Clear Quartz Crystal
Chakra: Solar plexus

- Develops higher wisdom, supports those in service to others and the planet
- Supports those on the Bodhisattva Path, aids teaching, relieves healers' burnout, rejuvenates
- Heals the light body, manifests karmic rewards

Healing Love Essence

———— ❈ ————

Flower: *Crape Myrtle (Lagerstroemia indica), pink*
Gemstones: *Kunzite, Rose Quartz, Pink Tourmaline,*
Danburite, Clear Quartz Crystal
Chakra: *Heart*

- Facilitates emotional body healing, heart healing
- Brings love into one's life
- Increases self-love, joy, forgiveness, trust, openness, calmness

Healing Victimization Essence

———— ❈ ————

Flower: *Pagoda Flower/ Claridendrum*
(Clarodendron speciosissimum), orange/red
Gemstones: *Carnelian, Red Spinel, Mexican Opal,*
Danburite, Clear Quartz Crystal
Chakra: *Root*

- Leads to sexual opening, supports balanced sexuality
- Strengthens spiritual relationships, brings security in relationships
- Helps to reject abuse and to leave abuse situations, heals victimization

Heart Essence

Flower: *Bougainvillea (Bougainvillea spp.), fuchsia*
Gemstones: *Pink Kunzite, Pink Tourmaline, Rose Quartz,*
Danburite, Clear Quartz Crystal
Chakra: *Heart*

- Strengthens body-mind-spirit connection, opens the heart, brings about heart healing and emotional body healing
- Allows individuality, free expression, and creativity; leads to inner harmony

Heart and Soul Essence

Flower: *Azalea (Rhododendron spp.), fuchsia*
Gemstones: *Cobaltite, Lepidolite, Rose Quartz,*
Danburite, Clear Quartz Crystal
Chakra: *Heart*

- Opens the heart, heals heart scars, heals past-life and this-life emotional wounds in heart chakra and aura layers
- Fosters karmic healing of emotional body, allows connection with oversoul
- Offers healing for heart dis-eases

Heart Clearing Essence

———— ❊ ————

Flower: *Ixora (Ixora coccinea), pink*
Gemstones: *Rose Quartz, Pink Tourmaline, Lepidolite,*
Danburite, Clear Quartz Crystal
Chakra: *Heart*

- Clears heart and emotional body of old this-life traumas, releases heart scars from this and past lives
- Heals emotional pain at the source
- Strengthens ability to give love to others and receive it, aids opening to others emotionally, increases learning to trust
- Alleviates heart dis-eases, palpitations, fear

Heart Warming Essence

———— ❊ ————

Flower: *Shell Ginger (Alpinea nutons), pink/white*
Gemstones: *Rose Quartz, Pink Kunzite, Pink Tourmaline,*
Danburite, Clear Quartz Crystal
Chakra: *Heart*

- Warms the heart, opens the heart after pain
- Brings emotional healing, grief recovery; releases old pain
- Brings about regeneration

Hera Essence

---- ❖ ----

Flower: Iris (Iris spp.), blue
Gemstones: Lapis Lazuli, Sodalite, Blue Aventurine,
Danburite, Clear Quartz Crystal
Chakra: Third eye

- Brings good fortune, promise of a better future
- Heals the negative past, clears the mental body of negative thought forms
- Stimulates courage to heal and change oneself, furthers emotional purification and mental growth
- Brings awareness of Goddess blessings and Goddess within
- Increases discernment, reduces stress

Holding Love Essence

---- ❖ ----

Flower: Floss-Silk Tree (Chorisia speciosa), pink
Gemstones: Gem Rose Quartz, Pink Fluorite, Moonstone,
Danburite, Herkimer Diamond
Chakra: Heart

- Heals and repairs the emotional body, astral body twin, and the heart chakra
- Heals one's relationships with oneself and others
- Aids learning to be with and cooperating with others in love and community situations
- Promotes learning to live together with a lover/mate
- Increases self-love, sustains holding love in one's heart at all times

Holy Blood Essence

———— ❖ ————

Flower: Chalice Vine *(Solandra nitida zucs.), maroon/cream*
Gemstones: Canadian Amethyst, Garnet, Mexican Opal,
Danburite, Clear Quartz Crystal
Chakra: Root

- Represents the sacred feminine, sacred womb; aids in transmission of the life force from mother to daughter to granddaughter
- Aids in transmission of women's mysteries through the generations, reveals the secrets of the Goddess and her women, teaches the rituals of the Goddess Craft
- Opens women's knowledge and psychic abilities, heals the blood and womb
- Promotes fertility, inspires ritual, aids in Drawing Down the Moon, strengthens connection with one's foremothers and the Goddess

Honesty Essence

———— ❖ ————

Flower: False Hibiscus/ Turkish Hats *(Malviavuscus arboreus), red*
Gemstones: Spinel or Ruby, Garnet, Pyrite, Danburite,
Clear Quartz Crystal
Chakra: Root

- Supports living on the earthplane; differentiates truth from falsehood, reality from illusion
- Encourages being truthful and honest, promotes competence in daily life, aids in making an honest living
- Helps anemia and blood dis-eases

Hope Essence

Flower: *Pandora Vine (Podranea ricasoliana), lavender/pink*
Gemstones: *Lepidolite, Pink Kunzite, Rutile Amethyst,*
Danburite, Clear Quartz Crystal
Chakra: *Heart*

- Engenders hope for one's life, trust in Goddess
- Repairs astral/emotional body aura, brings peace of mind and heart
- Supports emotional healing, leads to a feeling of calm and balance

Hui Yin Essence

Flower: *Torch Ginger (Alpinia purpurata), red*
Gemstones: *Red Spinel, Garnet, Black Tourmaline,*
Danburite, Clear Quartz Crystal
Chakra: *Perineum*

- Joins spiritual to physical life force, manifests life purpose
- Spiritualizes sexuality; enhances effort, courage, endurance, fertility
- Heals chronic fatigue, blood dis-eases, past sexual abuse, sexually transmitted dis-eases, depression

Hummingbird Essence

───── ❀ ─────

Flower: *Trumpet Creeper (Campsis radicans), red*
Gemstones: *Garnet, Amber, Azurite, Danburite, Herkimer Diamond*
Chakra: *Root*

- Attracts joy and brings it into one's life
- Clears and purifies kundalini and hara line obstructions preventing the manifesting of joy
- Heals sadness on emotional and mental body levels
- Connects with Goddess and Goddess within, brings one's higher self into physical energy
- Facilitates core soul healing and karmic healing, repairs twelve-strand DNA, aids the ascension process

Image Essence

───── ❀ ─────

Flower: *Prickly Pear (Opuntia spp.), yellow*
Gemstones: *Amber, Amber Calcite, Sunstone or Apatite, Danburite, Clear Quartz Crystal*
Chakra: *Hara*

- Gives the feeling of having a place in the world and a right to be here
- Calms, stabilizes, and soothes
- Improves self-image, creates a feeling of being wanted, helps a difficult adolescence
- Heals eating disorders, anorexia, overweight, digestive ulcers

Incarnation Essence

— ❀ —

Flower: Poinciana *(Delonix regia), red/gold*
Gemstones: Garnet, Ruby, Rutile Amethyst, Danburite, Herkimer Diamond
Chakra: Root

- Increases fertility, aids birth, strengthens will to live
- Strengthens the life force, activates twelve-strand DNA, heals karma
- Allows reincarnation in this lifetime, brings the soul-force into the body

Inner Change Essence

— ❀ —

Flower: Rose—Peace *(Rosa spp.), cream/pink*
Gemstones: Amber, Rose Quartz, Rutile Citrine, Danburite, Herkimer Diamond
Chakra: Hara

- Heals and balances all the hara line chakras and energy flows, stabilizes the kundalini heart chakra, fills the aura with light and healing
- Stabilizes during processes of intense change, life transitions, and deep healing; promotes a sense of courage, strength, and security during energy shifts
- Helps prepare one for change, aids trust in the process and in life

Inner Child Essence

Flower: Plumbago (Plumbago capensis), blue
Gemstones: Angelite, Blue Lace Agate, Kyanite,
Blue Aventurine, Clear Quartz Crystal
Chakra: Throat

- Aids in expressing emotional truths, releasing anger
- Facilitates inner child work, expands personal freedom, stimulates creativity, overcomes artists' block
- Furthers communication, increases inner peace, calms
- Heals headaches, migraines, sore throats

Inner Knowing Essence

Flower: Monks' Aster (Aster spp.), blue
Gemstones: Blue Lace Agate, Turquoise, Blue Aventurine,
Danburite, Clear Quartz Crystal
Chakra: Throat

- Clears blocks in throat, third eye, and thymus chakras
- Heals negative karma and releases karmic patterns, fosters understanding and expressing of karmic truths
- Enhances personal truth, fosters understanding and expressing of one's life purpose, increases certainty of one's path
- Reinforces inner knowing, brings inner peace, facilitates psychic opening and healing

Inner Light Essence

Flower: Rose—Garden Party (Rosa spp.), cream
Gemstones: Champagne Topaz, Amber, White Opal,
Danburite, Clear Quartz Crystal
Chakra: Crown

- Heals and balances all the kundalini line chakras and energy flows
- Fills the aura with light and healing; soothes, balances, and stabilizes aura energy
- Provides an emotional sense of security and assures one of being fully loved by other people and the Goddess
- Engenders trust in the universe and in the process of life, aids life transitions, teaches universal love

Inner Power Essence

Flower: Cassia Tree (Cassia spp.), yellow/pink
Gemstones: Rhodochrosite, Natural Citrine, Pink Kunzite,
Danburite, Clear Quartz Crystal
Chakra: Solar plexus

- Balances power in relationships; increases inner empowerment, a sense of Goddess within, self-confidence, self-love, inner strength
- Resists manipulation from others, aids in divorce process, allows leaving battered relationships, eases re-entry into single life

Intergalactic Essence

— ❀ —

Flower: Sweet Pea (Lathyrus odoratus), red
Gemstones: Garnet, Star Ruby, Labradorite, Danburite, Herkimer Diamond
Chakra: Perineum

- Brings awareness of one's life purpose onto the active physical level, helps manifest one's life path
- Brings consciousness of other realms and dimensions, aids transmitting and receiving conscious psychic information from positive other-planetary helpers and healers, aids channeling ascended spiritual Be-ings

Ishtar Essence

— ❀ —

Flower: Geranium (Geranium spp.), pink
Gemstones: Rhodochrosite, Pink Kunzite, Orange Calcite, Danburite, Clear Quartz Crystal
Chakra: Heart

- Allows one to become a priestess of the Goddesses of Love, increases ability to give and receive love, increases Goddess-within self-love
- Expands sensuality and sexuality, increases sexual excitement in relationship, deepens orgasm and sexual play
- Strengthens fidelity and monogamy in established relationships, builds a stable and responsible loving marriage

Isis Essence

───── ❀ ─────

Flower: Lignum Vitae / "wood of life" (Guaiacum officinales), blue
Gemstones: Lapis Lazuli, Malachite-Azurite, Eilat Stone,
Danburite, Clear Quartz Crystal
Chakra: Thymus

- Promotes all healing, self-healing; heals physical, mental, and light body levels
- Strengthens immune system, central nervous system
- Eases grief, restlessness, insomnia; heals trauma from past abuse
- Heals infections and wounds

Joy Essence

───── ❀ ─────

Flower: Canna (Canna xgeneralis striatus), red/gold
Gemstones: Mexican Opal, Amber, Carnelian,
Danburite, Clear Quartz Crystal
Chakra: Hara

- Fosters love of life; increases stability, vitality; furthers knowledge of life purpose
- Spiritualizes sexuality, aids depression, dissolves apathy, brings joy

Juno Essence

Flower: Lily—Calla (Zantedesclia spp.), yellow
Gemstones: Amber, Rutile Citrine, Sunstone, Danburite, Herkimer Diamond
Chakra: Hara

- Clears and purifies hara line energy channels, removes blocks and obstructions to personal and spiritual growth
- Aids all-aura cleansing and purification, fills the aura with light and healing
- Aids path to enlightenment and other positive spiritual paths, aids in manifesting one's life purpose successfully

Kali Essence

Flower: Rose—Royal Velvet (Rosa spp.), red
Gemstones: Garnet, Black Kyanite, Cinnabar Wood, Danburite, Clear Quartz Crystal
Chakra: Perineum

- Roots the incarnation and one's life purpose into the earth-plane, promotes a strong life purpose of service to the planet, makes one aware of her life purpose and intensifies will to accomplish it
- Aids those who are peaceful destroyers of evil and injustice
- Promotes clear intent, courage, and protection of goodness and truth

Kannon Essence

— ❧ —

Flower: Dahlia (Dahlia spp.), purple
Gemstones: *Rutile Amethyst, Canadian Amethyst, Sugilite,*
Danburite, Herkimer Diamond
Chakra: *Crown*

- Furthers spiritual growth and attainment, promotes the bodhisattva path, advances one on the path to enlightenment
- Helps those in service to the planet and people, supports healers and teachers
- Calms, soothes, and heals; aids psychic opening and development
- Aids stress; overcomes burnout, exhaustion, overwhelm, despair, and insomnia

Karma Essence

— ❧ —

Flower: Jacaranda (Jacaranda acutifolia), purple
Gemstones: *Sugilite, Canadian Amethyst, Lepidolite,*
Danburite, Clear Quartz Crystal
Chakra: *Crown*

- Clears karmic attachments and crown blocks, promotes understanding and releases karmic patterns
- Aids past-life work, channeling, accesses spirit guides, accesses the Lords of Karma and one's Akashic Records
- Boosts karmic and spiritual level healing, helps attain enlightenment in this lifetime

Kindness Essence

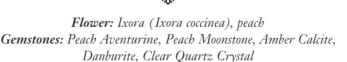

Flower: *Florida Honeysuckle (Bignonia), orange*
Gemstones: *Orange Calcite, Amber, Poppy Carnelian,*
Danburite, Clear Quartz Crystal
Chakra: *Belly*

- Heals painful memories and this-life traumas; eases emotional pain, body pain, fear, nightmares, panic attacks
- Helps arthritis and rheumatism
- Brings gentleness and kindness into one's life

Kundalini Cleansing Essence

Flower: *Ixora (Ixora coccinea), peach*
Gemstones: *Peach Aventurine, Peach Moonstone, Amber Calcite,*
Danburite, Clear Quartz Crystal
Chakra: *Belly*

- Cleanses the emotional and etheric bodies of old traumas by releasing flashbacks and "pictures"
- Facilitates incest recovery, aids recovery from battering and rape
- Helps recovery from past emotional and physical abuse, dissolves pain from old relationships
- Releases cords and hooks from Kundalini Line; supports, soothes, and calms

Kundalini Essence

Flower: Kapok Tree (Bomliax ceilia), red
Gemstones: *Elestial Quartz, Garnet, Black Kyanite,
Danburite, Clear Quartz Crystal*
Chakra: *Root*

- Strengthens uterus and ovaries, heals women's sexuality, eases menstruation
- Heals sexual abuse, stimulates orgasm
- Works to aid survival issues
- Increases love of living, fosters kundalini opening and stabilization, brings transformation

Kwan Yin Essence

Flower: Camellia (Camellia japonica), pink
Gemstones: *Kunzite, Pink Morganite or Rose Quartz, Aquamarine,
Danburite, Clear Quartz Crystal*
Chakra: *Heart*

- Brings healing and compassion into one's life; increases forgiveness, inner peace, self-esteem
- Engenders calm certainty, fosters heart healing
- Aids meditation, evokes Goddess love and Universal love

Life Essence

※

Flower: *Passion Flower (Passiflora spp.), red*
Gemstones: *Garnet, Cinnabar, Black Tourmaline,*
Danburite, Herkimer Diamond
Chakra: *Perineum*

- Enables living one's spirituality on the earthplane, grounds after psychic work
- Manifests one's life purpose, honors the oneness of all life
- Provides spiritual protection, releases attachments and entities, heals the life force

Life Blood Essence

※

Flower: *California Poppy (Eschscholzia calfornica), red*
Gemstones: *Garnet, Ruby, Red Quartz, Danburite, Clear Quartz Crystal*
Chakra: *Root*

- Stabilizes the life force, increases the will to live and continue
- Aids new infants and the critically ill
- Heals despair and overcomes the feeling of not wanting to be here
- Warms and stimulates, brings the soul force into physical levels
- Provides an emotional jump-start, increases vitality, cleanses red blood cells, and improves circulation

Life Force Essence

————— ❈ —————

Flower: *Torch Ginger (Nicolci elatior), red*
Gemstones: *Spinel, Garnet, Snow Quartz, Danburite,*
Clear Quartz Crystal
Chakra: *Perineum*

- Heals and warms the life force, increases the feeling of wanting to be here
- Balances soul and body, brings spiritual understanding of physical dis-ease
- Offers support in life threatening dis-ease, aids in healing blood dis-eases

Life Passage Essence

————— ❈ —————

Flower: *Rose—Oregold (Rosa spp.), deep yellow*
Gemstones: *Amber, Golden Topaz, Yellow Fluorite,*
Danburite, Clear Quartz Crystal
Chakra: *Solar plexus*

- Radiates a rainbow energy that clears, calms, and balances all the chakras
- Brings stability and inner peace after a process of change, sustains equilibrium
- Leads to recognition of new inner growth, increases joy and warmth within
- Promotes self-esteem, supports life transitions and completions, inspires emotional work well done

Light Essence

❀

Flower: Golden Chalice (Solandra nitida zucs.) or
Angel Trumpet Datura (Datura metel), yellow
Gemstones: Selenite, Clear Fluorite, Rutile Quartz,
Danburite, Clear Quartz Crystal
Chakra: Transpersonal point

- Allows opening to angels, devas, planetary guardians, other-planetary helpers and healers
- Brings connection with Earth and galactic grid, facilitates light body activation
- Aids Earth healing work; strengthens channeling, core soul healing; repairs twelve-strand DNA
- Brings energy/light activation, develops connection with Goddess and Goddesses

Light Body Essence I

❀

Flower: Gardenia (Gardenia jasminoides), white
Gemstones: Celestite, Moonstone, Danburite,
Herkimer Diamond, Clear Quartz Crystal
Chakra: Transpersonal point

- Heals, clears, and opens the light body
- Fosters core soul healing, heals soul fragmentation, repairs twelve-strand DNA
- Merges light body into physical level, accesses the oversoul
- Promotes ascension process

Light Body Essence II

Flower: Rose—Winchester Cathedral (Rosa spp.), cream white
Gemstones: Moonstone, Selenite, Mexican Opal,
Danburite, Clear Quartz Crystal
Chakra: Transpersonal point

- Opens and clears the transpersonal point, hara line, hara chakras, and galactic chakras
- Fills energy channels with light, prepares for entrance and anchoring of higher self
- Clears and heals the body of light, Ketheric and Celestial templates; aids core soul healing; repairs twelve-strand DNA
- Initiates, promotes, and aids ascension process

Lovers' Essence

Flower: Crape Myrtle (Lagerstroemia indica), dark red
Gemstones: Garnet, Pink Tourmaline, Pink Kunzite, Danburite,
Clear Quartz Crystal
Chakra: Perineum

- Manifests love on the earthplane, helps find one's soul mate
- Strengthens physical/spiritual relationships, increases opening to receive love
- Supports moving in and living together

Mary Essence

Flower: Camellia (Camellia japonica), pink/white
Gemstones: Rose Quartz, Pink Kunzite, Selenite, Danburite,
Herkimer Diamond
Chakra: Heart

- Heals the core soul, overcomes soul fragmentation, promotes astral body and light body healing
- Increases spiritual growth and transformation, inspires karmic grace and intervention
- Brings connection with the All-Mother, spirit guides, and angels
- Repairs twelve-strand DNA, promotes all healing, increases inner peace

Mary Magdalene Essence

Flower: Rose—Sonia (Rosa spp.), salmon pink
Gemstones: Pink Tourmaline, Kunzite, Lepidolite,
Danburite, Herkimer Diamond
Chakra: Heart

- Repairs and heals heart and emotional body, releases heart scars, dissolves long-term emotional pain
- Eases karmic pain; reduces loneliness, grief, helplessness, hopelessness
- Provides comfort, hope, patience, universal love, unconditional love

Maturity Essence I

———— ❈ ————

Flower: *Poinciana (Delonix regia), yellow*
Gemstones: *Moonstone, Natural Citrine, Golden Topaz,*
Herkimer Diamond, Clear Quartz Crystal
Chakra: *Solar plexus*

- Aids in overcoming shyness, helps in being who you are, furthers recognizing personal truths
- Aids transition from adolescence to adulthood
- Brings self-awareness, increases self-confidence, protects vulnerability

Maturity Essence II

———— ❈ ————

Flower: *Dwarf Poinciana (Poinciana pulcherrima), red/gold*
Gemstones: *Garnet, Amber, Red Jasper, Danburite,*
Clear Quartz Crystal
Chakra: *Hara*

- Manifests one's life purpose on the earthplane; brings spiritual maturity, sexual maturity; furthers coming of age
- Increases stability and responsibility, gives energy to achieve and succeed

Meditation Essence

Flower: *Tree Orchid (Bauhinia variegata), lavender*
Gemstones: *Sugilite, Rutile Amethyst, Pink Tourmaline, Danburite,*
Clear Quartz Crystal
Chakra: *Crown*

- Aids meditation, brings spiritual opening, increases compassion for all suffering
- Creates spiritualization of daily life, develops unconditional love, fosters spiritualized relationships
- Strengthens connection with guides and Goddess, awareness and contact with the Void and Nonvoid
- Heals the mental body, promotes the will to attain enlightenment in this lifetime

Menarche Essence

Flower: *Portulaca (Portulaca grandiflora), orange*
Gemstones: *Orange Calcite, Carnelian, Peach Moonstone,*
Danburite, Clear Quartz Crystal
Chakra: *Belly*

- Supports girls entering menarche and adolescence, furthers accepting and appreciating one's body
- Enhances self-image, increases self-love, manifests joy in being a woman
- Strengthens friendship with other girls, fosters good relationship with one's mother, assures opening to and understanding of early sexuality and sensuality
- Eases menstrual cramps and fears of menstruation

Mind Essence

———— ❀ ————

Flower: Jerusalem Thorn (Parkinsonia), yellow
Gemstones: Golden Topaz, Golden Beryl, Sunstone, Danburite,
Clear Quartz Crystal
Chakra: Solar plexus

- Heals and stimulates the powers of the mind; strengthens intellect, intuition, psychic awareness; enhances learning and creativity
- Fosters receptivity and self-awareness, brings openness to new ideas, promotes mental growth, stimulates mental body, aids astral travel

Mindful Heart Essence

———— ❀ ————

Flower: Rose—Redgold (Rosa spp.), pink/gold
Gemstones: Sunstone, Kunzite, Amber Calcite, Danburite,
Clear Quartz Crystal
Chakra: Solar plexus

- Balances will with compassion, inspires trust in Goddess
- Aids in learning to let go, facilitates surrendering the mind to the heart and soul
- Increases opening to emotion and one's feelings; brings emotional and mental stability, inner peace

Mind Travel Essence

———— ❖ ————

Flower: Morning Glory (Ipomea learu), blue
Gemstones: Blue Aventurine, Celestite, Lapis Lazuli, Danburite,
Clear Quartz Crystal
Chakra: Third eye

- Brings about travel to far places, other dimensions and planets; furthers mind and mental body expansion and healing
- Increases connection to the mind grid and Earth grid collective mind, allows contact with positive alien healers and teachers
- Aids mental communication and telepathy with people and animals, dolphin devas; expands psychic awareness; aids meditation

Moon Essence

———— ❖ ————

(Make on Full Moon by Moonlight)

Flower: Nightblooming Cereus (Cereus peruvianus), white
Gemstones: Moonstone, Lapis Lazuli, Azurite, Danburite,
Clear Quartz Crystal
Chakra: Third eye

- Connects with Goddess, enhances Goddess and moon ritual, Drawing Down the Moon
- Amplifies psychic work; aids contact with spirit guides, angels, and other positive discarnate helpers
- Provides protection; aids meditation; increases women's wisdom, moon wisdom
- Acts as an aphrodisiac

Moonflower Essence

(Make on New or Full Moon by Moonlight)

Flower: *Moonflower (Ipomoea), white*
Gemstones: *Peach Moonstone, Mexican Opal, Peach Aventurine,*
Danburite, Herkimer Diamond
Chakra: *Hara*

- Brings psychic information and awareness to conscious levels, aids psychic development
- Clears and opens the hara line chakras; facilitates contact with spirit guides, angels, and Goddess
- Brings stability of life purpose, aids in finding and achieving one's life path

Mother Kali Essence

Flower: *African Tulip Tree (Spathodea campanulata), red*
Gemstones: *Garnet, Black Velvet Tourmaline, Obsidian,*
Danburite, Herkimer Diamond
Chakra: *Perineum*

- Deals with issues of incarnation and death, karma and rebirth
- Clears entities and attachments, heals aura of negativity and evil, transmutes negative karmic patterns
- Dissolves anger and resentment, dispels negative thoughts

Mother's Essence

❈

Flower: Hibiscus (Hibiscus rosa sinensis), peach
Gemstones: Peach Moonstone, Champagne Topaz, Pink Coral,
Danburite, Clear Quartz Crystal
Chakra: *Belly*

- Increases fertility, aids conception, pregnancy, ensures healthy womb, brings easy delivery
- Helps with breast feeding
- Supports mothers, infants, children

New Beginnings Essence I

❈

Flower: Christmas Cactus (Schlumbergera zygocactus), white
Gemstones: Chrysoprase, Emerald, Green Fluorite, Danburite,
Clear Quartz Crystal
Chakra: *Heart*

- Brings emotional reopening after grief, loss, hurt, or disappointment
- Protects tenderness and vulnerability
- Aids new starts and new beginnings in life, eases convalescence and recovery on physical or emotional levels
- Provides courage, balance; aids shyness and fear; offers emotional protection

New Beginnings Essence II

———— ❀ ————

Flower: Christmas Cactus (Schlumbergera zygocactus), pink
Gemstones: Gem Rose Quartz, Pink Tourmaline, Red Phantom Quartz,
Danburite, Clear Quartz Crystal
Chakra: Heart

- Fosters healing and reopening from anger and pain, allows forgiveness and self-forgiveness
- Promotes gentle release of anger and resentment, aids letting go, increases compassion and universal love, brings inner peace
- Aids emotional rawness and recovery from pain, aids loving oneself and others again

New Beginnings Essence III

———— ❀ ————

Flower: Christmas Cactus (Schlumbergera zygocactus), red
Gemstones: Garnet, Red Coral, Black Kyanite, Danburite,
Clear Quartz Crystal
Chakra: Root

- Fosters healing and reopening after a broken relationship, sexual abuse, or battering
- Encourages reopening after pain to love again with new awareness, aids emotional recovery, allows new starts and new beginnings alone or with another
- Increases self-love, courage, strength, and balance
- Offers protection in vulnerable times of change

Old Soul Essence

—— ❀ ——

Flower: *Angel's Trumpet Datura (Datura metel), purple*
Gemstones: *Rutile Amethyst, Sugilite, Moonstone, Danburite,*
Herkimer Diamond
Chakra: *Crown*

- Provides understanding of the wheel of birth, death, and rebirth
- Promotes soul growth and transformation, aids in achieving one's life goals and learning
- Fosters maximum karmic growth, aids core soul healing, repairs twelve-strand DNA
- Supports bodhisattvas, old souls, and soul mates; brings enlightenment; encourages service

Oneness Essence

—— ❀ ——

Flower: *Passion Flower (Passiflora caereulea), purple/blue*
Gemstones: *Moonstone, Azurite, Kyanite, Angelite, Danburite,*
Clear Quartz Crystal
Chakra: *Third eye*

- Develops contact with Pleiadian wisdom, star wisdom; engenders oneness with all life and the universe
- Strengthens life purpose, increases universal love, aids psychic opening, evokes spirit guides, supports mediumship
- Aids meditation, dreamwork, calms

Opening Essence

———— ❀ ————

Flower: Lilac *(Syringa rulgaris), purple*
Gemstones: Rutile Amethyst, Sugilite, Lepidolite, Danburite,
Clear Quartz Crystal
Chakra: *Crown*

- Furthers openness to new people, situations, and things; increases flexibility
- Promotes acceptance of change, acceptance of spiritual growth
- Brings mental relaxation, aids meditation
- Alleviates neck and back pain, aids insomnia, reduces stress

Opening to Joy Essence

———— ❀ ————

Flower: Dipladenia *(Dipladenia splendens), pink/yellow*
Gemstones: Rhodochrosite, Cobaltite, Rose Quartz, Danburite,
Clear Quartz Crystal
Chakra: *Heart*

- Turns suffering into joy, allows letting go of the thought form that life has to be hard
- Releases suffering from one's life pattern, allows joy to enter and become one's life
- Lets go of anguish, karmic guilt, shame, and self-blame; focuses on receiving happiness

Oshun's Essence

Flower: Geranium (Geranium spp.), red
Gemstones: Garnet, Red Coral, Hematite, Danburite,
Clear Quartz Crystal
Chakra: Root

- Increases passion for life and love, brings the feeling of wanting to be here
- Stimulates high life force vitality
- Draws the right mate to you, fosters maturity in love and relationships, furthers realistic and balanced relationships
- Manifests aware marriage between same sex or opposite sex partners, encourages making a home together, brings sexual satisfaction
- Helps in bearing children or in developing other creativity together

Paradise Essence

Flower: Bird of Paradise (Strelitzia reginae), orange/blue
Gemstones: Amber, Mexican Opal, Brown Jasper, Danburite,
Clear Quartz Crystal
Chakra: Hara

- Focuses knowledge and intent of life purpose, protects free will
- Expands Hara Line and Kundalini channels, releases Hara obstructions
- Manifests life purpose in the world
- Aids women in abused relationships to break free
- Balances blood sugar

Patient's Essence

Flower: Rosebud Impatiens *(Impatiens spp.), red*
Gemstones: *Garnet, Red Spinel, Canadian Amethyst, Danburite,
Clear Quartz Crystal*
Chakra: *Root*

- Supports the life force in times of dis-ease, debility, exhaustion
- Builds patience in experiencing and waiting out an illness or dis-ease process
- Aids in recovery after surgery, strengthens and calms, helps worry and fear
- Aids blood loss, heals anemia, overcomes physical weakness

Peace Essence

Flower: Bluebird Vine *(Petrea valuhilis), light blue*
Gemstones: *Azurite, Angelite, Celestite, Danburite, Clear Quartz Crystal*
Chakra: *Throat*

- Calms; brings peace of mind, inner peace, happiness, contentment with life, wellness
- Fosters connection with guides, inner self, and oversoul; is all-healing

Pink Jewels Essence

———— ✻ ————

Flower: Shrimp Plant (Beloperone guttata), pink
Gemstones: *Gem Rose Quartz, Pink Tourmaline or Watermelon*
Tourmaline, Rutile Quartz, Danburite, Clear Quartz Crystal
Chakra: *Heart*

- Causes the heart to bloom with joy and love
- Heals heart scars gently, facilitates heart opening, eases heartache, heals heart dis-eases
- Promotes joy in living, accesses the Goddess Tara and Kwan Yin

Playful Essence

———— ✻ ————

Flower: Gazania (Gazania spp.), orange/red
Gemstones: *Carnelian, Mexican Opal, Sunstone, Danburite,*
Clear Quartz Crystal
Chakra: *Belly*

- Brings joy, happiness, peace of mind, love of life
- Increases vitality, self-confidence
- Promotes loving sexuality, playfulness

Prosperity Essence

———— ❊ ————

Flower: *Forsythia (Forsythia spp.), yellow*
Gemstones: *Peridot, Chrysoprase, Natural Citrine, Danburite,
Clear Quartz Crystal*
Chakra: *Solar plexus*

- Brings success, abundance, prosperity
- Increases ability to receive and ability to manifest
- Heals greed, envy, and jealousy; aids generosity
- Creates balance in spending and money management, encourages spending and saving wisely, balances fun in spending for oneself and for giving to others

Protection Essence I

———— ❊ ————

Flower: *Yarrow (Achillea), white*
Gemstones: *Moonstone, Pearl, Herkimer Diamond, Danburite,
Clear Quartz Crystal*
Chakra: *Transpersonal point*

- Manifests purity of spirit, gives spiritual protection
- Clears the aura; releases entities, attachments, and psychic attacks
- Offers safe spiritual growth, fills the aura with light

Protection Essence II

Flower: Yarrow (Achillea), yellow
Gemstones: Natural Citrine, Pyrite, Golden Topaz, Danburite,
Clear Quartz Crystal
Chakra: Solar plexus

- Protects from negative energy; repels and releases psychic attacks, negative entities
- Decreases jealousy, negative thoughts, and emotions
- Aids positive outlook under fire, acts as an antidepressant, increases courage, protects the curious

Psychic Balance Essence

Flower: Pandora Vine (Pandorea ricasoliana), red/white
Gemstones: Spinel or Ruby, Moonstone, White Calcite,
Danburite, Clear Quartz Crystal
Chakra: Third eye

- Balances spiritual and earthplane energy, aids psychic development, promotes psychic opening
- Supports being a psychic in the material world, validates one's psychic abilities and perceptions
- Eases returning to Earth after psychic work

Psychic Shield Essence

Flower: Rose—Gold Badge (Rosa spp.), yellow
Gemstones: Natural Citrine, Amber, Yellow Fluorite, Danburite,
Clear Quartz Crystal
Chakra: Solar plexus

- Balances and aligns energy, removes energy obstructions, removes psychic attacks
- Protects energy, offers all-aura protection, acts as a psychic shield, heals exposure to negative energy and interference
- Promotes right use of will, releases control by others and tendency to be controlling oneself
- Fills aura with light, peace, and healing

Pure Love Essence

Flower: Rose—Pascali (Rosa spp.), white
Gemstones: Selenite, Moonstone, Clear Quartz Crystal, Danburite,
Herkimer Diamond
Chakra: Transpersonal point

- Creates love and union, brings about union of body and soul
- Attracts true soul mates, aids light body and core soul healing, helps with soul fragmentation/soul retrieval, repairs twelve-stand DNA
- Inspires total trust in Goddess, in love, in the beloved, and oneself
- Brings inner peace, is all healing, fills the aura and all the bodies with light

Purpose Essence

———— ❈ ————

Flower: Chenille Plant (Acalypha hispida), red
Gemstones: Garnet, Hematite, Obsidian, Danburite, Clear Quartz Crystal
Chakra: Earth

- Grounds, calms, brings rootedness into incarnation
- Increases security, develops nurturance, brings a focus on one's life path, leads to knowing one's life path and knowing Mother Earth

Queen of the Night Essence

———— ❈ ————

(Make on Full Moon by Moonlight)

Flower: Queen of the Night (Selenicereus grandiflorus), white
Gemstones: Moonstone, White Opal, White Quartz, Danburite,
Herkimer Diamond
Chakra: Transpersonal point

- Increases connection with Goddess and the moon, helps in Drawing Down the Moon, accesses Goddess within
- Reinforces rituals of love, pleasure, and women; aids group energy, magick, meditation
- Increases sexual love, lesbian love; brings spiritual union; stimulates orgasm; unites astral and physical lovers

Rebalancing Essence

※

Flower: Stephanotis (Stephanotis jasminoides), white
Gemstones: Phenacite, Chrysoprase, Emerald, Danburite,
Clear Quartz Crystal
Chakra: Transpersonal point

- Calms and balances transitions and transformations; supports emotional, physical, and spiritual healing processes
- Aids mental repatterning, fosters core soul healing, smoothes life changes
- Promotes the ascension process and light body healing, soothes, insulates, comforts

Recovery Essence

※

Flower: Hibiscus (Hibiscus rosa sinensis), white
Gemstones: Moonstone, Rose Quartz, Pink Tourmaline,
Danburite, Clear Quartz Crystal
Chakra: Transpersonal point

- Aids in dealing with abandonment issues, eases loneliness, helps with alcohol recovery, deals with adult child issues
- Encourages self-determination, independence; increases self-worth; brings empowerment, oneness with all life

Relationship Essence

—— ❋ ——

Flower: Chain of Love/ Mexican Love Chain (Antigonon leptopus), pink
Gemstones: Pink Kunzite, Pink Tourmaline, Dioptase,
Danburite, Clear Quartz Crystal
Chakra: Heart center

- Attracts healthy relationships, supports being in relationship, builds new relationships, harmonizes living together
- Increases self-love, self-worth

Releasing Essence I

—— ❋ ——

Flower: Lantana (Lantana camara), pink/cream
Gemstones: Rhodochrosite, Pink Kunzite, Amber, Rose Quartz,
Danburite, Clear Quartz Crystal
Chakra: Heart and Solar plexus

- Stabilizes energy, accesses emotions, brings emotional release
- Calms, soothes present-life traumas, brings emotional rescue, releases stress, offers protection

(Use with orange Lantana, Releasing Essence II)

Releasing Essence II

—— ❀ ——

Flower: Lantana *(Lantana camara), orange/gold*
Gemstones: Amber, Amber Calcite, Natural Citrine, Danburite,
Clear Quartz Crystal
Chakra: Belly and Solar plexus

- Stabilizes energy, eases anxiety, connects emotions to their source
- Releases old traumas and pictures, facilitates emotional release, brings emotional rescue

(Use with pink Lantana, Releasing Essence I)

Releasing Essence III

—— ❀ ——

Flower: Lantana *(Lantana camara), lavender/white*
Gemstones: Sugilite, Amethyst, Purple Fluorite, Danburite,
Clear Quartz Crystal
Chakra: Crown

- Stabilizes energy, connects emotions to karmic source
- Opens and releases karmic emotional patterns, heals past life traumas and abuse
- Brings emotional rescue, spiritual calm; enhances understanding of one's life plan

Root Essence

———— ❋ ————

Flower: Hibiscus (Hibiscus rosa sinensis), red
Gemstones: Garnet, Ruby, Black Tourmaline, Danburite,
Clear Quartz Crystal
Chakra: Root

- Promotes sexual healing; aids healing from rape, battering, incest
- Strengthens life force, increases will to live, helps deal with survival issues
- Increases physical and emotional strength, protects, grounds, creates a feeling of being secure and in body

Rootedness Essence

———— ❋ ————

Flower: Allamanda (Allamanda spp.), chocolate
Gemstones: Smoky Quartz, Jet, Brown Jasper, Danburite,
Clear Quartz Crystal
Chakra: Grounding chakras

- Develops rootedness into the earthplane, grounds and centers
- Provides strength in walking one's life path, assures certainty of life purpose, promotes aura protection and repair
- Balances and harmonizes, stabilizes and steadies, focuses Earth awareness
- Helps in releasing addictions, eases withdrawal reactions

Sea Essence

Flower: Sea Oats (Chasmanthium spp.), green/tan
Gemstones: Green Aventurine, Peridot, Moonstone, Danburite,
Clear Quartz Crystal
Chakra: Heart

- Furthers attunement to the sea, Sea Goddess, and dolphins
- Balances body rhythms, menstrual rhythms; strengthens relationship to the moon
- Increases fertility, aids menopause, facilitates emotional body healing, calms

(Note: Sea Oats are a protected plant in many locations; it may be illegal to pick them.)

Self-Love Essence

Flower: Rose—Queen Elizabeth (Rosa spp.), pink
Gemstones: Pink Kunzite, Gem Rose Quartz, Kyanite with Lepidolite
(or Morganite), Danburite, Clear Quartz Crystal
Chakra: Heart

- Leads to positive self-image; increases self-esteem, self-worth, self-love, self-confidence
- Calms, brings emotional balance, inner peace
- Promotes balanced ability to give and receive, deepens compassion and forgiveness of oneself and others
- Draws love and universal love; is especially good for girls, adolescents, and those in recovery

Sexual Essence

— ❀ —

Flower: Flame Vine (Pyrostegiaignea), orange
Gemstones: Red Jasper, Carnelian, Mexican Opal, Danburite,
Clear Quartz Crystal
Chakra: Belly

- Deepens sexual love, stimulates orgasm, supports chosen fertility and conception
- Increases attraction between lovers, aids courtship, brings physical and spiritual union

Sexual Healing Essence

— ❀ —

Flower: Bolivian Sunsex (Curcuma spp.), orange
Gemstones: Orange Sunstone, Yellow Sunstone, Orange Calcite,
Danburite, Clear Quartz Crystal
Chakra: Belly

- Brings light and healing into the womb, facilitates sexual healing
- Heals sexual traumas, rape; aids incest recovery; heals trauma of sexual manipulation and abuse
- Helps recover from negative birth or giving birth experience
- Heals damage to uterus or vagina, helps with episiotomy and hysterectomy recovery
- Increases ability to enjoy sex and one's body, stimulates orgasm

Shield Essence

Flower: Yarrow (Achillea), multi—white, pink, yellow
Gemstones: Pearl, Amber, Lepidolite, Danburite, Clear Quartz Crystal
Chakra: Solar plexus

- Eases burnout, exhaustion; relieves fatigue; lessens vulnerability; reduces stress
- Shields chakras from negativity and psychic draining by others, protects and releases others' pain
- Is good for healers, social workers, activists, etc.

Shyness Essence

Flower: Spathiphyllum/ White Flag (Spathiphyllum spp.), white
Gemstones: Snow Quartz, Moonstone, Green Aventurine,
Danburite, Clear Quartz Crystal
Chakra: Third eye

- Overcomes shyness, vulnerability; offers protection, comfort in social situations
- Promotes emotional and spiritual growth, increases ability to reach out to others, helps during adolescence

Soul Retrieval Essence

———— ❁ ————

Flower: Rose—Brandy *(Rosa spp.), orange/peach*
Gemstones: Peach Moonstone, Peach Aventurine, Mexican Opal,
Danburite, Clear Quartz Crystal
Chakra: Belly

- Heals belly chakra and emotional body, aids in releasing past pictures of trauma and abuse from this life and past lives
- Heals the inner child and astral body twin, guides emotional reprogramming
- Aids in soul retrieval and healing soul fragments, facilitates core soul healing, offers emotional protection

Speaking Out Essence

———— ❁ ————

Flower: Hydrangea *(Hydrangea macrophylla), blue*
Gemstones: Lapis Lazuli, Celestite, Angelite, Danburite,
Herkimer Diamond
Chakra: Throat

- Releases what has long been unsaid, helps express personal truths
- Heals relationships through positive honesty; heals anger, depression, and rage
- Aids in letting go of past trauma, hurt, and pain by telling it
- Helps women in speaking personal herstories; inspires story telling, truth telling

Spinal Essence

Flower: Grapefruit Blossom (Citrus x. paradisi), white
Gemstones: White Opal, Pink Kunzite, Chrysocolla, Danburite,
Clear Quartz Crystal
Chakra: Third eye

- Aligns cranium and spine, eases back and neck pain
- Heals osteoporosis, arthritis, migraines, headaches
- Reduces stress, regenerates tissue
- Promotes clear thinking, balances chakras

Spiritual Blessings Essence

Flower: Hyacinth—Water (Eichbornia crassipes), lavender
Gemstones: Amethyst, Sugilite, Purple Fluorite, Danburite,
Clear Quartz Crystal
Chakra: Crown

- Brings spiritual blessings, inner growth, inner peace, spiritual nourishment, and fulfillment
- Fosters connection with Goddess, spirit guides, angels, and ascended Be-ings
- Promotes feeling held in the Goddess' arms, calms, aids trust
- Heals insomnia and fear, promotes peaceful death at time of transition

Spiritual Expansion Essence

— ✤ —

Flower: Impatiens (Impatiens sultanii), white
Gemstones: Selenite, White Phantom Quartz, Moonstone,
Danburite, Clear Quartz Crystal
Chakra: Transpersonal point

- Heals haste, anger, stress, and worry by releasing one from the limits of time and the mind
- Helps with entering the Void's bliss, transcends the material and the earthplane
- Increases spiritual awakening, clarifies awareness of what is and isn't important or real in life
- Sustains trust in the Goddess' nurturing and the Goddess' plan

Spirituality Essence

— ✤ —

Flower: Magnolia (Magnolia grandiflora), white
Gemstones: Moonstone, Rutile Amethyst, Sugilite, Danburite,
Clear Quartz Crystal
Chakra: Crown

- Leads to spiritual and psychic opening, aids in learning to meditate
- Brings connection with spirit guides and Goddess, furthers spiritual and psychic growth
- Engenders acceptance of a new way of Be-ing, allows experiencing of awareness levels beyond the physical, increases self-awareness

Stability Essence

Flower: *Rose—Bibi Maizoon (Rosa spp.), pink*
Gemstones: *Gem Rose Quartz, Pink Kunzite, Lepidolite, Danburite,*
Herkimer Diamond
Chakra: *Heart*

- Stabilizes and heals the heart and emotions, soothes and comforts
- Promotes and aids deep emotional change, releases and heals heart scars gently
- Heals the emotional body, astral twin, and inner child; facilitates core soul heart healing; promotes heart center repair and rescue; heals heart dis-eases
- Heals in layers from surface to depths

Star Essence

Flower: *Pentas (Pentas lanceolata), rose*
Gemstones: *Pink Kunzite, Cobaltite, Gem Rose Quartz,*
Danburite, Clear Quartz Crystal
Chakra: *Causal body chakra*

- Opens causal chakra, manifests star wisdom, deepens consciousness of universal truths
- Deepens consciousness of Earth and Universe, Goddess; fosters connection with star guides

Stargazer's Essence

— ❀ —

Flower: Lily—Stargazer (Lilium spp.), white/purple
Gemstones: Rutile Amethyst, Lepidolite, Watermelon Tourmaline,
Danburite, Clear Quartz Crystal
Chakra: Transpersonal point

- Inspires reaching for the stars, aids astrologers and astronomers
- Draws contact with intergalactic healers, contact with over-soul, other planets, and dimensions; facilitates astral travel

Star Goddess Essence

— ❀ —

Flower: Pentas (Pentas lanceolata), light pink
Gemstones: Gem Rose Quartz, Moonstone, Rutile Quartz,
Danburite, Herkimer Diamond
Chakra: Causal body chakra

- Aids in receiving Star Goddess wisdom; supports Wiccan ritual, the Goddess Craft, drawing down the stars
- Aids psychic work, channeling, astral travel; advances spirituality

Star Woman Essence

(Make on New Moon)

Flower: *Angel's Trumpet Datura (Datura suaveolens), peach*
Gemstones: *Moonstone, Labradorite, Azurite, Danburite,*
Herkimer Diamond
Chakra: *Transpersonal point*

- Increases Star wisdom and wisdom from other planets and dimensions
- Evokes Pleiadian, Goddess, spirit guides, and channeling
- Aids in soul level healing, repairs twelve-strand DNA, brings spiritual awareness

Strength Essence

Flower: *Heather (Cuphea glutinosa), purple*
Gemstones: *Amethyst, Rutile Amethyst, Moonstone, Danburite,*
Clear Quartz Crystal
Chakra: *Crown*

- Calms, offers spiritual comfort, soothes inner or outward chatter
- Eases anxiety and fear; increases spiritual strength, courage
- Fosters connection with guides

Stress Essence

———— ❊ ————

Flower: Rosebud Impatiens (Impatiens spp.), fuchsia
Gemstones: Pink Tourmaline, Cobaltite, Rose Quartz, Danburite,
Clear Quartz Crystal
Chakra: Heart

- Heals worry, stress, impatience; opens the heart to trusting life and the Goddess
- Promotes flowing with time and events, leads to understanding time as self-created by the mind, helps to live in the present peacefully
- Furthers trusting oneself, others, and the Goddess
- Clears up emotional sources of skin dis-eases

Success Essence

———— ❊ ————

Flower: Sunflower (Helionthus spp.), gold/brown
Gemstones: Sunstone, Amber, Brown Jasper, Danburite,
Clear Quartz Crystal
Chakra: Hara

- Balances spirit and body, aids in manifesting, creates abundance, success, self-confidence
- Encourages honesty, helps in achieving life purpose, aids in contribution to the world
- Promotes joyful living, good health

Sweetness Essence I

Flower: *Sweet Pea (Lathyrus odorata), lavender*
Gemstones: *Sugilite, Canadian Amethyst, Rose Quartz,*
Danburite, Clear Quartz Crystal
Chakra: *Crown*

- Increases the sweetness of life, tempers sadness with joy
- Brings spiritual certainty and security, engenders trust in Goddess
- Calms, brings restful sleep, eases fears and nightmares

Sweetness Essence II

Flower: *Sweet Pea (Lathyrus odorata), multi*
Gemstones: *Amber, Rose Quartz, Blue Lace Agate, Danburite,*
Clear Quartz Crystal
Chakra: *All the kundalini chakras*

- Aids chakra opening, stabilizes and balances energy
- Opens one to the joy and sweetness in one's life, creates heart opening
- Encourages learning to feel, trust, and speak out
- Deepens inner security and safety; engenders trust in Goddess, life, and oneself; brings inner peace

Tara Essence

———— ❀ ————

Flower: Camellia (Camellia japonica), white
Gemstones: White Phantom Quartz, Selenite, White Opal (or Labradorite),
Moonstone, Danburite, Clear Quartz Crystal
Chakra: Transpersonal point

- Helps in finding the Goddess, spirit guides, and angels; accesses Goddess within, advanced psychic healing and development
- Brings about core soul healing, heals soul fragmentation, repairs twelve-strand DNA, furthers ascension, heals the light body
- Produces contact with one's oversoul, brings enlightenment in this lifetime

Transcendence Essence

———— ❀ ————

Flower: Princess Flower Tree (Tibouchina semidecandra), purple
Gemstones: Ametrine, Rutile Amethyst, Purple-Yellow Fluorite,
Danburite, Clear Quartz Crystal
Chakra: Crown

- Aids in opening to Goddess/spiritual energy, helps in recognizing oneself as a spiritual Be-ing
- Connects with guides, angels, and Goddess; brings karmic healing
- Engenders trust in one's part in the universal plan, brings enlightenment in this lifetime

Transformation Essence

———— ❀ ————

Flower: Lobelia (*Lobelia chinensis*), *blue*
Gemstones: Lapis Lazuli, Malachite-Azurite, Angelite,
Danburite, Herkimer Diamond
Chakra: Brow

- Facilitates psychic opening and development, shatters emotional and mental barriers to growth and achievement
- Is all-healing; aids in gaining the assistance of spirit guides, angels, and Goddess in one's process of growth and change
- Aids in rebirthing, supports transformation on all levels

Transition Essence

———— ❀ ————

Flower: Lily—Easter (*Lilium spp.*), *white*
Gemstones: Golden Topaz, Amber, Selenite, Danburite,
Clear Quartz Crystal
Chakra: Crown

- Eases life changes and transitions, manifests peaceful dying
- Heals despair and fear, brings enlightenment, helps with letting go, sustains trust in Goddess

Trust Essence

Flower: Hibiscus (Hibiscus rosa sinensis), pink
Gemstones: Kunzite, Lepidolite, Gem Rose Quartz or Morganite,
Danburite, Clear Quartz Crystal
Chakra: Heart

- Heals betrayed trust and innocence, helps with rape and incest recovery
- Heals heart hurts, merges multiple personalities
- Eases pain of betrayed relationships and friendships, restores broken faith in life and the Goddess
- Offers calm and hope

Truth Essence

Flower: Mexican Blue Sage (Salvia hispanica), blue
Gemstones: Lapis Lazuli, Blue Aventurine, Azurite, Danburite,
Clear Quartz Crystal
Chakra: Throat

- Heals the voice; opens self-expression and creativity; aids singing, speaking, writing, art
- Furthers speaking one's truth, overcomes fear, supports asserting one's needs
- Increases honesty, honor, courage, tact, and wisdom; aids in speaking out

Unconditional Love Essence

———— ❀ ————

Flower: Clover (Trifolium), red
Gemstones: Watermelon Tourmaline, Kunzite, Gem Rose Quartz, Danburite, Clear Quartz Crystal
Chakra: Causal chakra

- Cleanses and clears emotional body, opens causal body chakra
- Connects with guides and angels, spiritualizes one's life and life purpose
- Aids mediumship, channeling; brings about knowing and giving unconditional love; deepens knowing Goddess

Unveiling Essence

———— ❀ ————

Flower: Clover (Trifolium), white
Gemstones: Moonstone, Phantom Quartz, Azurite, Danburite, Clear Quartz Crystal
Chakra: Vision chakras

- Allows seeing what must be seen, removes blocks from this and past lives, opens the veils revealing what is hidden
- Aids clairvoyance, mediumship, prophecy; increases knowledge about future lives
- Aids vision and eye disorders

Vision Essence

Flower: Nasturtium (Tropaeolum majus), cream or yellow
Gemstones: Blue Fluorite, Yellow Fluorite, Sugilite,
Danburite, Rutile Quartz
Chakra: Vision

- Balances left and right sides of the brain, focuses mind for learning and spiritual work
- Filters psychic static; aids channeling; strengthens mental effort, mental body
- Aids headaches, migraines; speeds neurological healing; heals vision disturbances; soothes mind chatter

Voice Essence

Flower: Mexican Blue Sage (Salvia hispanica), blue
Gemstones: Celestite, Blue Lace Agate, Holly Blue Agate,
Danburite, Clear Quartz Crystal
Chakra: Throat

- Heals dis-eases of throat and voice, cures karmic constrictions of throat and voice
- Aids ability to speak out, releases attachments and entities, fosters ability to express personal and spiritual truths
- Supports channeling, singing, teaching

Womb Essence

Flower: Lily—Tiger (Hemerocallis fulreia), orange
Gemstones: Orange Calcite, Red Jasper, Carnelian, Danburite,
Clear Quartz Crystal
Chakra: Belly

- Heals the womb, cervix, ovaries, and fallopian tubes
- Increases fertility, deepens sexuality, stimulates orgasm
- Heals past sexual abuse, encourages reaching out to others, helps in forming new relationship after sexual trauma
- Facilitates healing after hysterectomy, rape, or incest

Women's Balance Essence I

Flower: Frangipani (Plumeria rubra), pink
Gemstones: Lepidolite, Pink Tourmaline, Rutile Amethyst,
Danburite, Clear Quartz Crystal
Chakra: Heart

- Balances the female heart, fosters positive self-image, allows independent emotions
- Increases self-respect in relationships; aids healing from addictions, overeating, alcoholism, codependency, abuse, and past abuse; supports emotional healing

Women's Balance Essence II

———— ❀ ————

Flower: Frangipani (Plumeria rubra), yellow
Gemstones: Ametrine, Rutile Amethyst, Amber, Danburite,
Clear Quartz Crystal
Chakra: Solar plexus

- Promotes female mental balance, brings mental health and stability
- Increases self-respect, manifests success in the material world, brings work and job success
- Aids anorexia and eating disorders

Women's Body Essence

———— ❀ ————

Flower: Rose—Tropicana (Rosa spp.), orange
Gemstones: Vanadanite, Red Jasper, Carnelian, Danburite,
Clear Quartz Crystal
Chakra: Belly

- Promotes women's reproductive healing, aids infertility
- Furthers healing from sexual and physical abuse, aids rape recovery
- Brings about healing and rebalancing from reproductive surgery, helps menopause, heals fibroid tumors, acts as a hormone and emotional balancer

Women's Healing Essence

❀

Flower: Hibiscus *(Hibiscus rosa sinensis), red*
Gemstones: Garnet, Moonstone, Rutile Amethyst or Canadian Amethyst,
Danburite, Clear Quartz Crystal
Chakra: Root

- Supports female sexuality; heals sexual abuse; cures diseases of the uterus, ovaries, vagina, vulva
- Focuses on women's body issues, heals anorexia, acts as a women's all-healer
- Accesses Goddess within, the Great Mother

Zen Essence I

❀

Flower: Narcissus *(Narcissus tazetta), yellow*
Gemstones: Yellow Fluorite, Natural Citrine, Sunstone, Danburite,
Clear Quartz Crystal
Chakra: Solar plexus

- Helps in finding one's place in the physical world, brings self-confidence in earthplane activities
- Promotes working cooperatively with others, balances will and ego
- Strengthens focus on conscious daily life, manifests the Zen of living, reflects daily activity as a spiritual exercise, accesses pure mind

Zen Essence II

———— ❀ ————

Flower: *Narcissus—Paperwhite (Narcissus tazetta), white*
Gemstones: *Turquoise, Aquamarine, Moonstone, Danburite,*
Herkimer Diamond
Chakra: *Thymus*

- Brings harmony of inner and outer Be-ing, of daily and spiritual life
- Aids living as a conscious spiritual Be-ing in the world
- Aids clearing the emotions and emotional attachments
- Unclouds the mirror, reveals pure mind; aids those on the path to enlightenment and all spiritual paths
- Aids awareness of beauty and perfection in one's life

————————

Every flower is shouting at us of our common divinity, of our transcendent selves. We know it unconsciously. Our paradises have been gardens. We "say it with flowers." Our symbolic pictures of the universe, our manadalas, are flower designs. But now flowers are saying, with a new intensity, "Look, don't think; look directly at us and see God/dess."

Dorothy Maclean,
To Hear the Angel Sing:
An Odyssey of Co-Creation with the Devic Kingdom

FOOTNOTES

[1] Donna Cunningham, *Flower Remedies Handbook: Emotional Healing and Growth with Bach and Other Flower Essences*, (New York, Sterling Publishing Co., Inc., 1992), pp. 10–19.

[2] For detailed information on these experiments, see Peter Tompkins and Christopher Bird, *The Secret Life of Plants: A Fascinating Account of the Physical, Emotional, and Spiritual Relations Between Plants and Man*, (New York, Harper and Row Publishers, 1973).

[3] Bach Centre USA, *The Bach Flower Remedies*, (Woodmere, NY, Bach Centre USA, 1983), p. 4. And Diane Stein, *All Women Are Healers: A Comprehensive Guide to Natural Healing*, (Freedom, CA, The Crossing Press, 1990), pp. 234–235.

[4] Machaelle Small Wright, *Flower Essences: Reordering Our Understanding and Approach to Illness and Health*, (Jeffersonton, VA, Perelandra Ltd., 1988), pp. 58–61.

[5] The Twelve Chakras Diagram is based on information form Barbara Marciniak, *Bringers of the Dawn: Teachings from the Pleiadians*, (Santa Fe, NM, Bear & Co., 1992), pp. 55–56, and Barbara Marciniak, *Earth: Pleiadian Keys to the Living Library*, (Santa Fe, NM, Bear & Co., 1995), pp. 34–35.

[6] Barbara Ann Brennan, *Hands of Light: A Guide to Healing Through the Human Energy Field*, (New York, NY, Bantam Books, 1987), p. 47.

[7] The analysis of Carolyn Myss influences this version of the seven chakras. See C. Norman Shealy, MD and Carolyn M. Myss, MA, *The Creation of Health: The Emotional, Psychological and Spiritual Responses that Promote Health and Healing*, (Walpole, NH, Stillpoint Publishing, 1988, 1993), pp. 93–119.

[8] Barbara Marciniak, *Bringers of the Dawn*, p. 55–56, and *Earth*, pp. 34–35.

[9] Barbara Ann Brennan, *Light Emerging: The Journey of Personal Healing*, (New York, NY, Bantam Books, 1993), p. 29.

[10] Stephen Levine, *Healing Into Life and Death*, (New York, NY, Anchor Books, 1987), pp. 116–117.

[11] Cynthia Ahlquist, Ed., *Llewellyn's 1996 Organic Gardening Almanac*, (St. Paul, MN, Llewellyn Publications, 1995), pp. 296–297.

Flower Cross Reference

Name of Flower	Name of Essence
African Tulip Tree *(red)*	Mother Kali Essence
Allamanda *(purple)*	Aura Cleansing Essence
Allamanda *(yellow)*	Detox Essence
Allamanda *(chocolate)*	Rootedness Essence
Angel's Trumpet Datura *(peach)*	Star Woman Essence
Angel's Trumpet Datura *(purple)*	Old Soul Essence
Angel's Trumpet Datura *(white)*	Channeling Essence
Angel's Trumpet Datura *(yellow)*	Conscious Dying Essence
	Light Essence
Azalea *(white)*	Goddess Within Essence
Azalea *(fuchsia)*	Heart and Soul Essence
Bird of Paradise *(orange/blue)*	Paradise Essence
Bleeding Heart *(red/white)*	Bodhisattva Essence
Bluebird Vine *(light blue)*	Peace Essence
Blue Violet *(indigo)*	Clairvoyance Essence
Bolivian Sunsex *(orange)*	Sexual Healing Essence
Bottle Brush Tree *(red)*	Grounding Essence
Bougainvillea *(fuchsia)*	Heart Essence
Bougainvillea *(light pink)*	Birth Essence
Bougainvillea *(white)*	Aging Essence
Bromeliad *(pink)*	Forgiveness Essence
Bromeliad *(red)*	Anger Essence
Butterfly Weed *(orange)*	Flight Essence
California Poppy *(red)*	Life Blood Essence
Camellia *(pink)*	Kwan Yin Essence
Camellia *(white)*	Tara Essence
Camellia *(red)*	Aphrodite Essence
Camellia *(pink/white)*	Mary Essence

Candle Bush *(yellow)*	Golden Light Essence
Canna *(red/gold)*	Joy Essence
Cassia *(Rainbow)*	Family of Womon Essence
Cassia *(yellow/pink)*	Inner Power Essence
Century Plant *(orange)*	Courage Essence
Chain of Love *(pink)*	Relationship Essence
Chalice Vine *(maroon/cream)*	Holy Blood Essence
Chalice Vine *(yellow)*	*see* Golden Chalice
Chenille Plant *(red)*	Purpose Essence
Chinese Lantern *(yellow)*	Fairy Essence
Christmas Cactus *(white)*	New Beginnings Essence I
Christmas Cactus *(pink)*	New Beginnings Essence II
Christmas Cactus *(red)*	New Beginnings Essence III
Christmas Plant *(red/green)*	Blood Building Essence
Claridendrum *(orange/red)*	Healing Victimization Essence
Clematis *(dark blue)*	Energy Purification Essence I
Clematis *(dark red)*	Energy Purification Essence II
Clover *(red)*	Unconditional Love Essence
Clover *(white)*	Unveiling Essence
Confederate Jasmine *(white)*	Beloved Essence
Cosmos *(multi)*	Blessing Essence
Crape Myrtle *(pink)*	Healing Love Essence
Crape Myrtle *(dark red)*	Lovers' Essence
Crape Myrtle *(lavender)*	Devotion Essence
Crape Myrtle *(white)*	Eternity Essence
Crossandra *(orange)*	Cassandra Essence
Cuban Buttercup *(yellow)*	Assimilation Essence
Dahlia *(purple)*	Kannon Essence
Dandelion *(yellow)*	Cleansing Essence
Diplodenia *(pink/yellow)*	Opening to Joy Essence
Dwarf Poinciana *(red/gold)*	Maturity Essence II
False Hibiscus *(red)*	Honesty Essence
Flame Vine *(orange)*	Sexual Essence

Florida Honeysuckle *(orange)*	Kindness Essence
Floss-Silk Tree *(pink)*	Holding Love Essence
Forsythia *(yellow)*	Prosperity Essence
Frangipani *(red)*	Amazon Essence I
Frangipani *(white)*	Amazon Essence II
Frangipani *(pink)*	Women's Balance Essence I
Frangipani *(yellow)*	Women's Balance Essence II
Gardenia *(white)*	Light Body Essence I
Gazania *(orange/red)*	Playful Essence
Geranium *(pink)*	Ishtar's Essence
Geranium *(red)*	Oshun's Essence
Geranium *(white)*	Hathor's Essence
Gladiolus *(pink)*	Gladness Essence
Gloxinia *(fuchsia)*	Earth Love Essence
Gloxinia *(maroon/white)*	Earth Walk Essence I
Gloxinia *(purple/white)*	Earth Walk Essence II
Golden Chalice *(yellow)*	Conscious Dying Essence
Golden Chalice *(yellow)*	Light Essence
Golden Rain Tree *(yellow)*	Abundance Essence
Grapefruit Blossom	Spinal Essence
Heather *(purple)*	Strength Essence
Hibiscus *(multi colors)*	Chakra Essence
Hibiscus *(red)*	Women's Healing Essence
Hibiscus *(red)*	Root Essence
Hibiscus *(white)*	Recovery Essence
Hibiscus *(yellow)*	Aura Essence
Hibiscus *(peach)*	Mother's Essence
Hibiscus *(pink)*	Trust Essence
Hollyhock *(white)*	Acceptance Essence
Honeysuckle *(pink)*	Deva Essence
Hyacinth *(blue)*	Awareness Essence
Hyacinth *(red)*	Earth Changes Essence
Hyacinth *(white)*	Ascension Essence

Hyacinth-Water *(lavender)*	Spiritual Blessings Essence
Hydrangea *(blue)*	Speaking Out Essence
Impatiens *(white)*	Spiritual Expansion Essence
Iris *(blue)*	Hera Essence
Ixora *(red)*	Blood Cleansing Essence
Ixora *(yellow)*	Ch'i Kung Essence
Ixora *(pink)*	Heart Clearing Essence
Ixora *(peach)*	Kundalini Cleansing Essence
Jacaranda *(purple)*	Karma Essence
Jacobena *(pink)*	Easy Essence
Kapok Tree *(red)*	Kundalini Essence
King's Mantle *(purple/gold)*	Channeling Essence II
Lantana *(pink/cream)*	Releasing Essence I
Lantana *(orange/gold)*	Releasing Essence II
Lantana *(lavender/white)*	Releasing Essence III
Lignum Vitae *(blue)*	Isis Essence
Lily—Calla *(yellow)*	Juno Essence
Lily—Easter *(white)*	Transition Essence
Lily—Spider *(white)*	Creation Essence
Lily—Stargazer *(purple/white)*	Stargazer Essence
Lily—Tiger *(orange)*	Womb Essence
Lilac *(purple)*	Opening Essence
Lisianthus *(purple)*	Comfort Essence
Lobelia *(blue)*	Transformation Essence
Magnolia *(white)*	Spirituality Essence
Mandevilla *(pink)*	Changing Woman Essence
Mexican Blue Sage *(blue)*	Truth Essence
Mexican Blue Sage *(blue)*	Voice Essence
Monk's Aster *(blue)*	Inner Knowing Essence
Moonflower *(white)*	Moonflower Essence
Morning Glory *(indigo)*	Mind Travel Essence

Narcissus *(yellow/white)*	Harmony Essence
Narcissus *(yellow)*	Zen Essence I
Narcissus *(white)*	Zen Essence II
Nasturtium *(cream or yellow)*	Vision Essence
Nightblooming Cereus *(white)*	Moon Essence
Orange Blossom *(white)*	Cupid Essence
Pandora Vine *(lavender/pink)*	Hope Essence
Pandora Vine *(red/white)*	Psychic Balance Essence
Parkinsonia *(yellow)*	Mind Essence
Passion Flower *(purple/white)*	Oneness Essence
Passion Flower *(red)*	Life Essence
Pentas *(rose)*	Star Essence
Pentas *(light pink)*	Star Goddess Essence
Peony *(white)*	Grief Essence
Pink Poui Tree	Happiness Essence
Plumbago *(blue)*	Inner Child Essence
Poinciana *(yellow)*	Maturity Essence I
Poinciana *(red/gold)*	Incarnation Essence
Portulaca *(pink)*	Children's Essence
Portulaca *(fuchsia)*	First Love Essence
Portulaca *(orange)*	Menarche Essence
Portulaca *(yellow)*	Clarity Essence
Portulaca *(mixed colors)*	Circus Essence
Powder Puff *(red)*	Body and Soul Essence
Prickly Pear *(yellow)*	Image Essence
Princess Flower Tree *(purple)*	Transcendence Essence
Queen of the Night *(white)*	Queen of the Night Essence
Rose—Angel Face *(lavender/pink)*	Angelic Grace Essence
Rose—Bibi Maizoon *(pink)*	Stability Essence
Rose—Brandy *(orange/peach)*	Soul Retrieval Essence
Rose—Climbing Tea *(pink)*	Good Old Days Essence
Rose—Garden Party *(cream)*	Inner Light Essence

Rose—Gold Badge *(yellow)*	Psychic Shield Essence
Rose—Oregold *(yellow)*	Life Passage Essence
Rose—Pascali *(white)*	Pure Love Essence
Rose—Peace *(cream/pink)*	Inner Change Essence
Rose—Perfume Beauty *(pink)*	Astarte Essence
Rose—Queen Elizabeth *(pink)*	Self-Love Essence
Rose—Redgold *(pink/gold)*	Mindful Heart Essence
Rose—Reine des Violettes *(purple)*	Crown Essence
Rose—Royal Velvet *(red)*	Kali Essence
Rose—Sonia *(salmon pink)*	Mary Magdalene Essence
Rose—Tropicana *(orange)*	Women's Body Essence
Rose—Winchester Cathedral *(white)*	Light Body Essence II
Rosebud Impatiens *(fuchsia)*	Stress Essence
Rosebud Impatiens *(red)*	Patient's Essence
Sea Oats *(green/tan)*	Sea Essence
Shell Ginger *(pink/White)*	Heart Warming Essence
Shrimp Plant *(yellow)*	Golden Jewels Essence
Shrimp Plant *(pink)*	Pink Jewels Essence
Shrimp Plant *(white)*	Crown Jewels Essence
Shrimp Plant *(white)*	Green Jewels Essence
Silk Oak Tree *(orange)*	Hara Essence
Sky Vine *(blue)*	Brede's Essence
Sky Vine *(white)*	Ariel's Essence
Sky Vine *(white)*	Angel Essence
Spathiphyllum *(white)*	Shyness Essence
Sunflower *(gold/brown)*	Success Essence
Sweet Pea *(lavender)*	Sweetness Essence I
Sweet Pea *(multi)*	Sweetness Essence II
Sweet Pea *(red)*	Intergalactic Essence
Torch Ginger *(red)*	Life Force Essence
Torch Ginger *(red)*	Hui Yin Essence
Tree of Gold *(yellow)*	Healer's Essence
Tree Orchid *(lavender)*	Meditation Essence

Trumpet Creeper *(orange)*	Emotional Essence
Trumpet Creeper *(yellow)*	Energy Essence
Trumpet Creeper *(red)*	Hummingbird Essence
Water Lily *(white)*	Enlightenment Essence
Water Lily *(white)*	Earth Essence
Water Lily *(purple)*	Ancient Wisdom Essence
Water Lily *(indigo)*	Galaxy Essence
Wisteria *(blue)*	Archangel Essence
Yarrow *(white)*	Protection Essence I
Yarrow *(yellow)*	Protection Essence II
Yarrow *(pink)*	Astral Essence
Yarrow *(multi—white, pink, yellow)*	Shield Essence
Yesterday, Today & Tomorrow *(blue)*	Forever Essence

Bibliography

Ahlquist, Cynthia, Ed. *Llewellyn's 1996 Organic Gardening Almanac*. St. Paul, MN: Llewellyn Publications, 1995.

Bach Centre USA. *The Bach Flower Remedies*. Pamphlet. Woodmere, NY: Bach Centre USA, 1983.

Brennan, Barbara Ann. *Light Emerging: The Journey of Personal Healing*. New York, NY: Bantam Books, 1993.

Brennan, Barbara Ann. *Hands of Light: A Guide to Healing Through the Human Energy Field*. New York, NY: Bantam Books, 1987.

Cunningham, Donna. *Flower Remedies Handbook: Emotional Healing and Growth with Bach and Other Flower Essences*. New York, NY: Sterling Publishing Co., Inc., 1992.

Findhorn Community, The. *The Findhorn Garden: Pioneering a New Vision of Man and Nature in Cooperation*. New York, NY: Harper and Row Publishers, 1975.

Levine, Stephen. *Healing Into Life and Death*. New York, NY: Anchor Books, 1987.

Maclean, Dorothy. *To Hear the Angels Sing: An Odyssey of Co-Creation with the Devic Kingdom*. Elgin, IL: Lorian Press, 1980.

Marciniak, Barbara. *Earth: Pleiadian Keys to the Living Library*. Santa Fe, NM: Bear & Co., 1995.

Marciniak, Barbara. *Bringers of the Dawn: Teachings from the Pleiadians*. Santa Fe, NM: Bear & Co., 1992.

Bibliography continued

Shealy, C. Norman, MD and Carolyn M. Myss, MA. *The Creation of Health: The Emotional, Psychological and Spiritual Responses that Promote Health and Healing.* Walpole, NH: Stillpoint Publishing, 1993.

Stein, Diane. *Healing with Gemstones and Crystals.* Freedom, CA: The Crossing Press, 1996.

Stein, Diane. *Natural Healing for Dogs and Cats.* Freedom, CA: The Crossing Press, 1993.

Stein, Diane. *All Women Are Healers: A Comprehensive Guide to Natural Healing.* Freedom, CA: The Crossing Press, 1990.

Sunset Books. *Garden Pests and Diseases.* Menlo Park, CA: Sunset Publishing Group, 1993.

Tompkins, Peter and Christopher Bird. *The Secret Life of Plants: A Fascinating Account of the Physical, Emotional and Spiritual Relations Between Plants and Men.* New York, NY: Harper and Row Publishers, 1973.

Wright, Machaelle Small. *Flower Essences: Reordering Our Understanding and Approach to Illness and Health.* Jeffersonton, VA: Perelandra Ltd., 1988.

Essential Essences

Essential Essences mother tinctures have been personally prepared by Diane Stein from flowers grown in her own garden, with gemstones from her personal collection. Essential Healing Circle, Inc. is working with Diane Stein to offer essences based on her research. The following is a list of the essences which are available.

Flower Essences
Angel Essence
Angelic Grace Essence
Ariel's Essence
Astarte Essence
Aura Essence
Aura Cleansing Essence
Beloved Essence
Brede's Essence
Changing Woman Essence
Channeling I Essence
Channeling II Essence
Detox Essence
Healing Love Essence
Hope Essence
Inner Change Essence
Inner Child Essence
Kali Essence
Life Essence
Light Body Essence
Lover's Essence
Mary Magdalene Essence
Mind Travel Essence
Moonflower Essence
Old Soul Essence
Oneness Essence
Psychic Shield Essence
Pure Love Essence
Star Woman Essence
Transcendence Essence

Flower Essences cont.
Trust Essence
Women's Body Essence
Women's Healing Essence

Gemstone Essences
Amber Essence
Amethyst Essence
Angelite Essence
Aquamarine Essence
Aventurine Essence
Azurite Essence
Celestite Essence
Citrine Essence
Clear Quartz Crystal Essence
Dioptase-Malachite Essence
Elestial Quartz Essence
Emerald Essence
Herkimer Diamond Essence
Jasper Essence
Kunzite Essence
Kyanite Essence
Lapis Lazuli Essence
Moldavite Essence
Moroccan Red Quartz Essence
Phenacite Essence
Rose Quartz Essence
Selenite Essence
Tourmaline Essence
Vanadanite Essence
Zincite Essence

Each essence is available in a 1/2 ounce bottle with a dropper top. We perserve them in a brandy base unless distilled white vinegar is requested. To receive a copy of the Essential Reiki Journal with a price list and order form please send a check for $3.00 to:

The Essential Reiki Journal
P.O. Box 1436
Olney, Maryland 20830-1436

OTHER BOOKS BY DIANE STEIN

Psychic Healing with Spirit Guides and Angels
This book presents a complete program of soul development for self-healing, healing with others, and Earth healing. Many of the methods included in this book have never before been published. Advanced skills include healing karma and past lives, soul retrieval, releasing entities and spirit attachments, and understanding and aiding the death process.
$18.95 • Paper • 0-89594-807-9

Essential Reiki: A Complete Guide to an Ancient Healing Art
While no book can replace the directly received Reiki attunements, *Essential Reiki* provides everything else that the healer, practitioner, and the teacher of this system needs, including full information on all three degrees of Reiki, most of it in print for the first time.
$18.95 • Paper • 0-89594-736-6

The Natural Remedy Book for Women
This best-seller includes information on ten natural healing methods—vitamins and minerals, herbs, naturopathy, homeopathy and cell salts, amino acids, acupressure, aromatherapy, flower essences, gemstones and emotional healing. Remedies from all ten methods are given for fifty common health problems.
$16.95 • Paper • 0-89594-525-8

Grief and Dying: Understanding the Soul's Journey
Guiding the reader on a healing journey to a place of loving acceptance, this book offers comfort and help to persons facing death and to those who love them.
$15.00 • Hardcover • ISBN 0-89594-830-3

OTHER BOOKS BY DIANE STEIN

All Women Are Healers: A Comprehensive Guide to Natural Healing
A wealth of "how-to" information on various healing methods including Reiki, reflexology, polarity balancing, and homeopathy, intended to teach women to take control of their bodies and lives.
$14.95 · Paper · 0-89594-409-X

Natural Healing for Dogs & Cats
Tells how to use nutrition, vitamins, minerals, massage, herbs, homeopathy, acupuncture, acupressure, and flower essences, as well as owner-pet communication and psychic healing.
$16.95 • Paper • ISBN 0-89594-614-9

The Natural Remedy Book for Dogs & Cats
The perfect companion to Stein's earlier book- Natural Healing for Dogs and Cats. Fifty common pet ailments and remedies are arranged in alphabetical order. Methods of treatment including nutrition, naturopathy, vitamins and minerals, herbs, homeopathy, acupuncture/acupressure, flower essences, and gemstones are discussed for each illness.
$16.95 • Paper • ISBN 0-89594-686-6

Casting the Circle: A Women's Book of Ritual
$14.95 • Paper • 0-89594-411-1

The Goddess Celebrates: An Anthology of Women's Rituals
Contributors include Z. Budapest, Starhawk, and others.
$14.95 • Paper • 0-89594-460-X